WILDWOOD'S
Neon Nights & Motel Memories

Melinda M. Williams
and Robert O. Williams

Cover design by Randy Hentges of A.B.S. Sign Company and Christine McIntire of The Williams Group.
Front Cover- The Pink Champagne Motel has everything a Wildwood Motel would ever want. From its dramatic street corner sign to the bathing glow of pink on every surface at night this beauty is timeless. Located on Atlantic Avenue a block south of Rio Grande Avenue in Wildwood. The Caribbean Motel at night is a dance of living color. No other motel in Wildwood quite captures the '60's vibe like this treasure.
Back Cover- The pool at the Caribbean Motel.
Title Page- The Caribbean Motel at 5600 Ocean Avenue in Wildwood Crest is on the National Register of Historic Places. The original sign was created by Harry Lanza of Allied Lanza Sign Company.

Every effort has been made in this book to be accurate and factual. Any errors, omissions or inaccuracies were not the intention of the author or publisher.

Library of Congress Control Number: 2010923110

Designed by Mark David Bowyer
Type set in HarlowD / Zurich BT

ISBN: 978-0-7643-3479-5
Printed in China

Schiffer Books are available at special discounts for bulk purchases for sales promotions or premiums. Special editions, including personalized covers, corporate imprints, and excerpts can be created in large quantities for special needs. For more information contact the publisher:

Published by Schiffer Publishing Ltd.
4880 Lower Valley Road
Atglen, PA 19310
Phone: (610) 593-1777; Fax: (610) 593-2002
E-mail: Info@schifferbooks.com

For the largest selection of fine reference books on this and related subjects, please visit our web site at
www.schifferbooks.com
We are always looking for people to write books on new and related subjects. If you have an idea for a book please contact us at the above address.

This book may be purchased from the publisher.
Include $5.00 for shipping.
Please try your bookstore first.
You may write for a free catalog.

In Europe, Schiffer books are distributed by
Bushwood Books
6 Marksbury Ave.
Kew Gardens
Surrey TW9 4JF England
Phone: 44 (0) 20 8392 8585; Fax: 44 (0) 20 8392 9876
E-mail: info@bushwoodbooks.co.uk
Website: www.bushwoodbooks.co.uk

Contents

The Panoramic Motel, 2101 Surf Ave., North Wildwood.

Dedication

The 1957 Chevy Bel Air in original Inca Silver paint, owned by Fred Frieze Jr. of Boothwyn, Pennsylvania, glides west on Rio Grande Avenue. As Fred and his family depart town, the new Wildwood Sign gleams in the background after a fall rain. Fred has had this beauty with its ivory top for twenty-one years.

To my parents, Edward and Claire Campitelli, who showed me the world from the back seat of their Chevrolet Impala.

—Melinda Williams

And to our son, Gregory, who saw that same world, 30 years later, from the back seat of our Ford Explorer.

—Melinda M. Williams and Robert O. Williams

Acknowledgments

We extend our deepest gratitude and most sincere appreciation to the following people who made the completion of this book possible:

Our entire family, network of friends and business colleagues who paved the way for us and encouraged the completion of this book. Team members of The Williams Group, especially Christine McIntyre and Kirsten McCurdy. Ann Moore for editing my treatise with patience and love. Bob Hentges for being a 'walking encyclopedia' of Wildwood sign knowledge. Carolyn Travis, Dan MacElrevey and David Bard. Ed and Claire Campitelli for getting us to the shore every summer. Edward J. Campitelli for his support, research, and being a sounding-board for our project. Eric Bard for preserving his father's legacy and his generosity. Fred Musso for being our very first Wildwood connection and never being afraid to share all of his knowledge with us.

Gregory Williams for being the best, most innovative and loving child any parent could ever desire. Gordon Clark for his graciousness, helpfulness and unending hospitality.

Jack Morey for his kindness, openness and hospitality. Jeff Wooten, editor of *Sign Builder Illustrated Magazine*, who took us on our first two "editorial" trips to Wildwood. Jeral Hentges for 'getting the job done'! Joanne Vitali for forcing to me to focus. Jo and Janet Casaccio who made every day seem like summer. Kirk Hastings for his fact-filled book on Wildwood, *Doo Wop Motels*. The Koren Family, Lindsey Young for her perpetual smile and 'can-do' attitude. Max and Heidi for their unequivocal love and patience.

Philadelphia Inquirer friends: Larry Kesterson, Jim Seltzer, Dan Z. Johnson, and Gloria Hoffner. Lori Gitterman for her loyal friendship and support.

Randy Hentges, of A. B. S. Sign Company for his design for the cover, unending graciousness, patience and expertise. Richard Stokes for enlightening me about the nuances of Mid-century architecture. Rick Campitelli for occupying my childhood days with adventure, fun and love. Shirley Cruz, who was an invaluable resource of information. Simmons-Boardman Publishing for selected passages of this book that, "originally appeared in *Sign Builder Illustrated Magazine.*" Terry O'Donnell for rental of his "little red house." The George F. Boyer Museum (Wildwood Historical Society), especially Ann Vinci for her superlative detective skills and Bob "Brighty" Bright for his deep knowledge of Wildwood and unending patience.

The following people for being magnanimous enough to share their Wildwood Stories with us: Edward Campitelli, Sally Campitelli, Brian McCullough, Maryann Riviello, Kirsten McCurdy, Catherine McDaniel, Barbara Travaglini, Becky Reeves, Bob Eldredge, Marc Turner, Lou Rodilico, Paul Martone, Helen Mason, and Christina Campitelli.

Our special thanks to the City of Wildwood, Wildwood Crest, North Wildwood and West Wildwood and all of their residents.

And to editors Tina Skinner and Nancy Schiffer at Schiffer Publishing for taking the chance on us and our project.

Introduction

Robert O. Williams

The first time I drove into Wildwood, I was nearly twenty-one years old in 1978. In fact, I am ashamed to admit that until that time, I had never stepped into the Atlantic Ocean either. I was a small town boy whose vacations usually took place within a hundred-mile radius of my upstate New York home. When I first laid my eyes on the Wildwood strip with my then girlfriend, Melinda Campitelli (now my wife), I was awestruck. It was my version of *Lost in Translation*. I knew not what a hoagie or a Wawa was, and "Yo" was half of a kid's toy to me, not a greeting. Driving into Wildwood was akin to the scene in the *Wizard of Oz* when the movie jumps from black & white to Technicolor.

I was a guy whose past vacations consisted of either summers at a Boy Scout Camp or a week with my parents at a rustic Adirondack Lake lodge. We did live dangerously once or twice by visiting neighboring Vermont or by jumping over the Canadian border near the St. Lawrence Seaway. Apparently, my parents had gotten the entire world-traveling thing out of their system by the time I came along. The culture shock of Wildwood was intimidating to a kid who was used to motels with names like Big Pine, Deerhead Lodge, the Lakefront Inn, and Bald Mountain Motel, not to mention every other outpost named after a proud Native American tribe that inhabited upstate New York.

Looking south on Ocean Avenue past the Crusader Motel.

Wildwood was the world in five square miles. You could arrive at the Beach Colony and then venture to the European shores of Barcelona and Florence. You hopped over a couple streets and you had arrived in a Polynesian village. The best value for me was the trip into space at the Astronaut or the ever-exciting Satellite Motel. The name Eden Roc was lost on me, having never been to Miami, but not the tailfin styling of the motel's façade.

I guess I should mention that along the way I was also a novice photojournalist, who at the time was chasing fires and a job. I eventually landed at *The Philadelphia Inquirer* where I honed my craft over the next 22 years. Those first few visits to Wildwood were more about a boy and a girl than taking photographs. As a young couple, we were into discovering America. We would set our sights on Florida, California, the Midwest and New England. Fast-forward down the road and we had our son, Gregory, in 1990. We needed to put on the brakes and take vacations that were more manageable with a baby. The Jersey Shore was an ideal fit. We liked Cape May and we would slowly venture back to Wildwood via the boardwalk over the next several years.

During the early 1990s, I took a leap of faith and started to work on my first book, *Hometown Diners*. I loved the stainless steel diner that was the town hall of culinary delights. It was a photographer's paradise. I drove up and down the east coast chasing every imaginable incarnation of the American eatery. I met the most amazing people who ran these temples of comfort food. Though they owned a real piece of history, a treasure of architectural splendor, more often than not, they worried most about putting their kid through college or paying the mortgage. As they prepared heart-warming, belly-filling delights for the soul, the architectural significance of their 1952 Mountain View diner was on the back burner. The diner world was a cast of characters who also struggled to find the balance between preservation and simply allowing the diner to do what it was meant to, serve delicious food at reasonable prices. The most original diners were often the lucky (or unlucky) product of neglect, which means they had not been renovated and all their original parts were still intact. Richard Gutman, the foremost diner authority in America, has spent the last twenty-five years saving diners and educating the public about their significance. The movement has spared many diners from the wrecking ball, but preservation is a delicate balance. This all translates to similar icons, such as the single-screen movie palace, the drive-in movie or the Wildwood Doo Wop Motel.

Astronaut Motel, 511 E. Stockton Rd., Wildwood Crest.

The Beach Holiday Motel, 239 E. Pine Ave.,Wildwood.

MaryAnn Motel, 421 E. 23rd St., Wildwood.(demolished).

I can be a pretty fair photojournalist, but I am the first to admit the best stories are the ones right under our noses; the ones we have ignored because we are a bit too anxious for the "big story" that sets the world upside down. As I pursued diners, drive-in movies and Roadside Americana, I missed the cues each summer as I vacationed at the shore. We would take our son to the boardwalk for rides on Morey's Pier and eat Curley's Fries. I would also steal a few moments to grab some shots of the neon signs that I realized were incredibly awesome.

The turning point belongs to my eagle-eye son, Gregory, and my wife, Melinda. They were driving down Pacific Avenue on a day that I was back in Philly working, and spotted the then de facto home of the Doo Wop Museum. It was an old storefront containing dozens of neon signs, architecturals and random salvages from Wildwood's bygone days and tumultuous present. On hand was Fred Musso, one-half artist and the other half preservationist.

He toured my family around this "funhouse" and the salvage yard out back. Melinda could barely contain her enthusiasm and called me as soon as she exited the building. She e-mailed me several grainy snapshots telling me, "You have to see this place!" Suffice it to say I contained my enthusiasm for a couple of weeks, but when I finally got there my eyes opened and I was forever changed. Standing in front of me was Wildwood like I had never seen her before. Wildwood had offered me a second chance to appreciate its place in time as a unique architectural treasure trove that just happened to be located on one of the finest beaches in North America.

Over the next couple of years, the very generous Fred Musso toured me around Wildwood pointing out its treasures and missteps. He told me stories of missed opportunities to save a sign or a valiant save as the wrecking ball swung. I was quick to observe that preservation was not always a welcome neighbor at every business. Preservation cost money that was hard earned. At the same time, I learned about efforts of the renowned architect Steve Izenour (sadly, now deceased) and the design studio groups from Kent State, Yale and the University Of Pennsylvania's School of Architecture. They had come, at Steve Izenour's request, to evaluate Wildwood's relevance to architecture. The folks in Wildwood were not sure what they had, but never fathomed they were sitting on the mother-load of Mid-century architecture. Wildwood was ready for a metamorphosis. The renaissance had begun, and with it came speculation.

At seasons' close in 2004 and 2005, the fleets of dump trucks marching in and out of town were like a line of ants and signaled the great teardown of mom and pop motels that never could be replaced. I begged my newspaper to let me photograph this transition. The rain poured as I watched the bulldozer push over the walls of places like The Tally Ho, The Bonanza and The Carousel. I listened to whispers about which motel had sold and which would be next for final vacancy.

When the dust cleared, a multitude of the classic motels met their demise, and in their place were erected orderly rows of 3- or 4-story condominium units that had all the modern amenities, including a garage. This was not some evil conspiracy, but a fact of capitalism. The owners of the classic motels had poured their hearts and souls into their Doo Wop Motel. They paid their bills, raised their kids, and were getting tired of the maintenance. They pushed their children to be doctors, lawyers, and teachers, but probably last on their list of potential careers was motel owners. When a developer offered them a check for a million or two, it was a no-brainer. Here was a well-earned retirement and probably a legacy more tangible to give their children. Let's be honest, every motel torn down was not a treasure and change is necessary for progress. The problem was, viable motels with significant architectural relevance also met the wrecking ball because the checkbook was out and the ink was flowing.

Ebb Tide Sign, (motel demolished, sign still remains).

Wildwood, however, still has the greatest collection of motels and signage in the Doo Wop style, period. Eyes are now open wide and the response by businesses in Wildwood is to embrace the past to ensure the future. As I photographed the motels, signs, and people who make Wildwood what it is, I was comforted by the knowledge that I was not alone. I was far from alone. For example, I knew the Doo Wop Preservation League was saving signs and entire buildings, but I did not know how much the business community was involved.

The Morey family not only owns amusements but also motels in Wildwood. They do not run their business from a Manhattan high-rise, but rather from offices overlooking The Big Wheel on Morey's Pier. They care about Wildwood, and by example have inspired others also to care. Traditional businesses, like Wawa, Acme and Harley Davidson (among others), have embraced Doo Wop without ever losing sight of good business. In fact, it is good for business!

My introduction is not a soapbox from which to pontificate. My response was to do what I do best, document the here and now, because it could soon be part of the past. This book is a testimonial to a thriving community, not a struggling one. The best way to support the preservation of the past is simply to enjoy the present. Stay at the motels in Wildwood, ride the roller coasters, play the games of chance, walk the mile-wide beach, eat Curley's Fries on the boardwalk and provide your family with memories that will last forever. Wildwood will do the rest.

Walk on the Wild Side

"I want to thank you for giving me the most wonderful summer of my life..."

The 1960s were an interesting time to be a kid. The proverbial saying, "Everything was simpler then," was unequivocally true. Life was divided into three segments; school, play time and summer vacation. It was that simple. Nothing else mattered. And, as good as playtime was, summer vacation was much better!

Our summer vacations were set in a "Levittown" (the quintessential planned community of the 1950s) -kind of place called Del Haven, New Jersey. During the mid- to late 1960s, it was a rather new development of two- and three-bedroom bungalows halfway between Cape May and Wildwood, New Jersey, situated about a mile from the Delaware Bay. My parents spent the money they had recently received from my departed grandmother's estate to buy the $5000 house in Del Haven. Well, life was good! Or, as good as it got for struggling, middle-class, suburban-dwellers who wanted a summer vacation.

All I knew was that I got to spend the entire summer "down the shore." The fact that my father worked in the city all week and my mother was not a driver did not affect me originally. But eventually, I caught on. I caught on very quickly, in fact, when I realized I was 'stuck' in this little town in the middle of nowhere— without even a 7-Eleven or gas station nearby! Did I mention we did not get a phone until three years later? We were isolated from the world, or so it seemed. The nearest body of water was the Delaware Bay, to which my brother and I would make a trek every day: I for the possibility of swimming and he for the possibility of catching fish. Neither intention would ever be realized. There was no swimming available there, it was filled with jellyfish and horseshoe crabs, and most importantly was the absence of lifeguards. Every morning the dead carcasses of crabs and jellyfish would litter the beach.

One of my dearest friends, Janet Casaccio (Guthrie), and me proving that we survived the Hell Hole! Photo taken by Josephine Casaccio

It was only during our attempts to 'analyze' the dead that we realized they were not dead at all, just caught on the wrong side of the tide going out too quickly. Their grotesque, wiggling clawed legs would feverishly reach for the sky or perhaps my tender young fingers! And fishing? Well, my brother never caught anything, except more horseshoe crabs, for whatever excitement there was in that. Yet still, we went there regularly, hoping perhaps for a different outcome with the dawn of each new day.

But Friday, beloved Friday, could not come quickly enough for our little family. It was those glorious Friday nights when my father drove down in his '58 Chevy Impala station wagon (sometimes with my eldest brother in tow) and a car filled with groceries and treats (like a giant brick of New Yorker Cheese and potato chips). On those nights, I would plead to go to the children's paradise to our north, Wildwood-By-The-Sea. Usually my father was tired from work, tired from his drive and already tired from my mother's litany of 'events' of the week. He rarely granted me the pleasure of going to "the boardwalk of boardwalks." "Work before play," he used to emphasize. However, sometimes, just sometimes, when the planets were in perfect alignment and when all was right with the universe, we would go to Wildwood.

Beyond a magical place in the late 1960s and early 1970s, Wildwood was the stuff that dreams were made of. Even as a kid, I sensed a certain 'edginess' to the town, yet it only fueled my excitement for it, instead of diminishing it.

The Lollipop Motel at 2301 Atlantic Avenue is the motel sign that captivates the heart and releases those childhood memories. Designed By Harry Lanza of Allied Lanza Sign Company.

Rio MOTEL
WILDWOOD'S FINEST
DIRECTLY ON THE BEACH
NEW JERSEY'S NEWEST OCEAN-FRONT RESORT MOTEL
ROOMS and STUDIO APARTMENTS
As new as tomorrow, as comfortable as yesterday . . . this is vacation pleasure at its very best, "where the end of the road meets the ocean." The new Rio Motel invites you to enjoy the matchless informality of delightful, spacious studio rooms and efficiencies. . . full luxury appointments . . . smart and new with every convenience for supreme vacation pleasure.
PARK AT YOUR DOOR
On "The World's Finest and Safest Bathing Beach!"
The invigorating surf is warmed to 72° by the nearby Gulf Stream.
Phones: 2-8198 - 2-2004 - 2-5831

The Rio Motel brochure had all the right answers for the perspective summer guest.
Courtesy of The Wildwood Historical Society

Unlike Cape May, which I would not come to appreciate fully until I was a full-fledged adult, Wildwood was...well...'wild'! There was nothing like it anywhere I had ever been. My Dad's government job afforded my Mom and me the opportunity to travel with him occasionally (on the cheap) on business trips. Therefore, I had 'been around' a little bit. I had been to Miami Beach and other similar places, but they were certainly not Wildwood. I remember sitting in the backseat of my dad's steel-blue Chevrolet Impala station wagon with my chin pressed up against the door ledge looking in amazement at the lights, because after all, it was that gas-infused glow and dazzling architecture that truly set this place apart from every other. You could seemingly drive for miles and see nothing but motels rimmed in purple, aqua, sea foam green and yellow neon lights and tubular strips. Light years later, when I would drive through Las Vegas, I still did not get the same 'feel' I got when I was in Wildwood. Its "Jetson-esque" architecture and the neon-lit atmosphere commanded a world all its own.

In the 1960s, fluorescent tubular strips and colored incandescent lights illuminated outer hallways of motels (visible from the street) to create a distinctive lighting pattern. To those not familiar with this, you may recall the fluorescent tubular lighting (usually honey yellow) at roadside rests or ice cream stands in the country. One could never determine if they lured in the bugs or repelled them. In Wildwood, it was usually neon, fluorescent tubing, incandescents and the seminal stages of rope lighting.

Wildwood took this concept and elevated it with the diverse use of color (a lot of purples, pinks, aquas and yellows) and application (they were on every inner railing, roofline and fascia board, giving the entire motel a 'lit up' appearance). Even the ugliest motels (although to me there were no ugly motels in Wildwood) looked exotic in the glow of colored lights! Use of this technique was not lost on many owners.

However, most notable of all things "illuminating" were the neon signs themselves. Block after block, each motel seemed to try to outdo one another with the height, scope and breadth of their signage.

Some signs were small and sat at street level, while others were large, all encompassing, and sat at the very top of the motel. The Nor'easter storms loved these signs best of all, ripping them apart with evil abandonment. Some motels had it all, a small street-level sign to attract the car owners or foot traffic (who walked in the '50s and '60s?) and then a grander sign that usually displayed the motel's logo. A large logo sign was plastered on a broad exterior wall as well. Interestingly, it was the sign that built the logo, not the logo that built the sign. Unlike marketing plans of today, a logo was not designed and then applied to all collateral materials (letterhead, business cards, brochures, signs, etc.). Back then, they designed the sign first, and from that image the logo was born and everything else followed suit.

From a kid's perspective, this type of signage and architecture was only seen on Saturday morning cartoons featuring George Jetson and his boy, Elroy. Remember those "out-of-this-world" signs? Who could forget Orbit High School, Skypad Apartments or Spacely Sprockets? On the other hand, if you had been lucky enough to travel to Disneyland or Disney World and visited "Tomorrowland," it indeed had a very familiar look. There were many corkscrew ramps, airport hanger roofs, crinkle-cut (or multi-prowed) rooflines, cantilevered porches and coffee shops. Many of the trendy little motels featured sting-ray-like flying wings, ascending ramps and ports, not to mention the ribbons of multi-colored lights that lit each floor, railing and roofline. Color was so intense it blurred your vision! Greens, yellows, pinks, corals, aqua's—did I mention yellow?

Unlike its Victorian neighbor, Cape May, three miles down the coast, Wildwood was a different place entirely. The post-war boom saw many new motels built on undeveloped beach land. These had traded-in static architecture for lines with movement, like the automobile era that it was mirroring. Wildwood was on the move and the buildings bore every sign of it.

Back then, I did not have a clue what Doo Wop, Populuxe, or Googie styles meant. I later found out that Wildwood's architecture was the "little sister" of a style out in California made famous in the 1940s, called Googie. Doo Wop attempted to mirror it, and *Populuxe* (a book) was a fabricated name by former *Inquirer* columnist, Thomas Hine, used to describe the "fabulous fifties and early sixties." The name Googie was coined for a coffee shop on Sunset Boulevard of the same name, which architect John Lautner designed. The name "Googie" would eventually stick like glue to that style of architecture and become its own culture. The culture, like many art forms before their time, was never appreciated until years and years later, when we were already starting to tear it down.

Googie, it is argued, mirrored not only America's love affair with the automobile at the time (think big tailfins, arched hoods and streamlined roofs), but the great space race which was already captivating the country. Once Sputnik was launched in 1957, space was literally "all the rage." The generic name for Googie is Mid-century Modern or Commercial Modernism. This application was usually seen on everything from a coffee house (a movement all its own) to gas stations, bowling alleys and, of course, motels! When you think of Googie, think of the shapes of "Tomorrowland" with boomerangs, criss-crossing planetary orbits, atoms, parabolas, amoeboids, dingbats, cheeseholes, woggles and bean poles!

I would later learn that the Googie-inspired applications I knew in Wildwood took some fascinating and exhilarating forms! It was the dynamic, in-motion structural attributes (and the sheer proliferation of buildings all in one place) that truly set Wildwood's architecture apart from the rest. It felt more like a "spaceport" than a "resort" at any given time.

If the architecture did not pull you in, the plastic palm trees and flora did. Even as a kid, I knew it was not "quite right," but that did not douse my enthusiasm for it! The up lights on the gently swaying palms almost made them look real. Who knew that they took the fronds down every winter and left just the trunks?

Yet, I think it was the names that really sold me—the wild, crazy names of the motels. Even though it was not Florida, the Caribbean or French Polynesia, the themes of the motels gave you that feeling anyway. Wildwood instantly transported you to places like Miami Beach, Hawaii or the Caribbean with motel names such as the Eden Roc, Pan American, the Royal Hawaiian, the Tahiti, the Kona Kai and the Caribbean. On the other hand, perhaps it was "Space: the Final Frontier" that tickled your fancy? Then stay at the Satellite, the Twilight or the Stardust. World travel set you afire? How about the Hialeah, Imperial 500, Ocean Holiday, the Bel Air or The San Souci?

Somehow, telling the folks back home that you stayed at the Eden Roc was far more compelling than saying, "I stayed at the Motel 9." The names had panache, appeal and allure. They somehow made you feel as though you were "someplace far, far away" on vacation, not just "down the shore."

What good was an intriguing name if you did not have a bold, traffic-stopping neon sign to scream it out? Outside of Las Vegas, Wildwood had to be the home of some of the most classic examples of Mid-century neon signage that ever existed in this country—signs right out of a set-designer's sketch-pad. These signs were a perfect amalgam of kitsch and class. Many of them now exist only in our collective memory and in faded photographs.

Each little motel vied for its place on the strip with a fabulous and unusual illuminated sign. One sign was more eye-catching than the next. Each was multi-colored and intricate, and most were neon, featuring prancing carousel horses, giant lollipops with children's faces, sweeping tidal waves, and people climbing out of suitcases or palm trees. Each was more beautiful than its predecessor was. Sometimes a very small motel with a very large sign would win a guest over. Of course, to a kid, the fact that Wildwood had a two-mile boardwalk complete with the world's greatest amusement piers only enhanced the experience.

The neon glow of Wildwood could be seen for miles around. It was like a luminescent anemone on the ocean floor, glowing brilliantly through the blanket of night. It was perhaps a phosphorescent haze that illuminated the shoreline like a line of fire. This beautiful light came from the many 'strips' of motels Wildwood proffered. There were many strips, as opposed to "one," because the beach kept getting wider (from street to ocean), every year.

This was especially true after "The Winter Storm of 1962," which devastated the area for three full days. In addition, the road that originally edged the water (Ocean Avenue) did not edge the water any longer. "That's why," as Jack Morey told *Wildwood Days* producer Carolyn Travis, "when you drive down Ocean Avenue, on the right side of the street there are the '50s motels and on the left side are the '60s motels."

Under the Boardwalk...

It is an intriguing fact that almost anyone you speak to who has had some experience on the Jersey shore has indelible memories of Wildwood. In addition, those memories are as diverse as the people proffering them, whether it was about the vintage motels, the immense boardwalk, "coming of age" experiences or the "adventure" of being in Wildwood. A place unlike any other, not only lost in itself but able to make its inhabitants feel that way as well.

The Strand Movie Theater on the Boardwalk in Wildwood was once one of a half-dozen movie houses in Wildwood. It shows summer blockbusters and romantic comedies, as if Wildwood did not have enough action or romance already. 3100 Boardwalk.

Aside from the Ocean Avenue strip, the main attraction in Wildwood was, without question, its sensational, two-mile boardwalk. The smells, sights, sounds and tastes of the boardwalk are indelibly etched in my mind forever. I can still smell the sausage, peppers and onions frying (an Italian favorite), the smell of hot oil frying the twirled funnel cakes, the sweetness of cotton candy, and the acrid smell of the amusement machines that jam-packed every arcade, all mixed with the saltiness of the ocean breeze.

The shark eats the arrow on this killer sign for the Seaport Aquarium. A.B.S. Sign Company of Wildwood built this tongue & cheek stunner. 3400 Boardwalk.

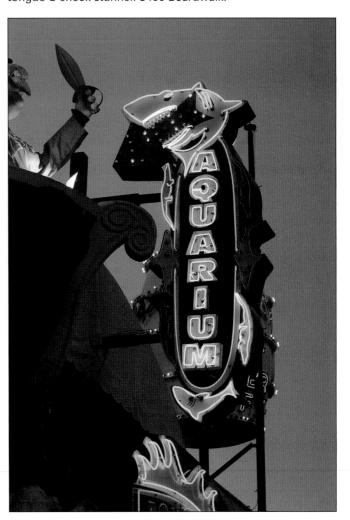

The Strand Movie Theater "S" is a perfect perch for a seagull.

Bobby Dee's Casino is where games of chance require nothing more than a pocketful of quarters and patience to lose a few times before they call you a winner. The sign's neon coins jingle as they beckon you in. 3600 Boardwalk.

15

And the sights of the Boardwalk? Well, let us just say it is a photographer's haven. You will see virtually every kind of person, in every kind of attire, doing the craziest, laughter-inspiring things in the middle of the boardwalk - at any time of day. It is a true people-watcher's paradise!

The sounds of the boardwalk were usually an assault on the ears, most notably the "Watch the tram car, please" recording that warned you that you had just seconds to move before being run over by "The Sightseer," a little open-air tram that traversed the entire boardwalk for just a couple of bucks. Game buzzers seemed to surprise you from every angle and, of course, there were hawkers who promised you, "Everyone's a winner!" The sounds I remember most about the boardwalk are the music—loud, blaring music that represented the audience of the day. I especially remember Three Dog Night's *Joy To The World* pounding on my ear drums as we rode back and forth on The Trabant (a circular ride, that took passengers up and back over a series of "hills" or "waves," faster and faster on every loop).

Laura's Fudge at Wildwood And Ocean Ave. is technically not on the boardwalk. A quick hop down the ramp and your hunger for delicious fudge is satiated. If you don't know the address, you sure can't miss the traveling sign.

With all the temptations to eat along the boards, the Nut Hut offers a healthy alternative. Located at 3210 Boardwalk.

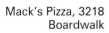

Mack's Pizza, 3218 Boardwalk

18

Talk to anyone who's ever been to Wildwood and they will recall the cheesy goodness of Mack's Pizza, the slithery cool of a Kohr Brothers Frozen Custard, the chocolate richness of Laura's Fudge and the salty satisfaction of The Nut Hut's roasted peanuts!

I still remember my Wednesday afternoons on the Wildwood boardwalk of the early 1970s. My mother and I would take the bus from Del Haven (usually standing the entire trip since Del Haven was at the end of the route) and be deposited at the Oak Avenue bus depot.

Flipper's Fascination, 4104 Boardwalk, Wildwood

The DooWop Diner has more than this great sign going for it. If Doo Wop has a taste as well as a sound, this is the place. 4010 Boardwalk.

"Watch The Tram Car Please".

From there, we would make our way up onto the boardwalk, where we would catch a movie at The Ocean Theater (I recall *True Grit* with John Wayne being especially action-packed). Afterwards, we would eat lunch at Pierre's (where I'd have a cream cheese and olive sandwich) and stop into Douglass Fudge to be drenched in their ice-cold air conditioning and get a little treat for the bus ride home. Right before we'd catch the bus back to Del Haven, I would have a few minutes for a game of nickel pitch, a game in which I was a master (the one and only)! Nickel pitch consisted of a smooth, glass-like surface, just a foot off the ground, painted with daisies. If you 'pitched' your nickel and hit any part of the flower, you were a winner! I usually hit the petals (scoring a nice little candy dish or something similar for my Mom), but once, only once, I hit the center and took home "The Grand Prize," a giant St. Bernard dog! I kept that dog for years as a symbol of my winning ability! My parents finally had to throw it out after I was married and had children of my own.

"Through This Arch Walk The Happiest People In The World." The boardwalk begins and ends at this arch in North Wildwood. A companion arch greets you in Wildwood Crest.

The Wonderless Years

Before the advent of the tumultuous 1980s, it is only right that we pay homage to a sign shop that came into full thrust during the 1970s, called Allied Lanza. Harry Lanza owned Allied Lanza Sign Company. He was athletic, energetic, Italian and utterly creative. His skills in commercial art yielded some of the finest and most recognizable designs in all of Wildwood (and up and down the southern New Jersey coast). Think of Harry when you think of the giant sprawling script of The Caribbean Motel or the giggling faces of the children in the lollipops of The Lollipop Motel. Did the Zaberer's sign make you salivate? Thank Harry! He also designed other memorable giants, such as the Madrid, the Commodore, the V.I.P., the Pan-Am and the Mid-Towne. Not to mention, almost all of the signage on Hunt's Pier and their other properties.

But perhaps the project that Harry was most proud of was his work on Diamond Beach. Anyone who spent any time at all in Wildwood remembers the beckoning arches of the Diamond Beach resort, at the southern end of the island. Harry (who sadly, passed away in 1993) is remembered fondly by his son, Wayne Lanza, an electrical engineer out of Melbourne, Florida. "A million years ago, Diamond Beach was massive. It had a theater in there, meeting rooms, ballrooms and a lot more. It was a huge facility! Dad was extremely proud of his work at Diamond Beach, especially with the two arches and the roof-top sign. At the time, Diamond Beach was 'the elite' in sign building, with its stainless steel cases and intricate neon work. Dad would smile with pride every time we visited that part of town."

V.I.P. Motel, 6505 Atlantic Ave. at Forget Me Not Road, Wildwood Crest.
Sign created by Harry Lanza of Allied Lanza Sign Company

Yet, as beautiful as Harry's work was, it was not enough to keep Wildwood on the radar of finicky tourists. With the blur of the 1980s, 1990s and turn-of-the-new century came big changes for the southern Jersey shore. Most of the other seaside communities south of Atlantic City were "turning condo," while Atlantic City itself began rolling the dice. In 1976, Cape May had been christened a National Historic Landmark and became a romance seeker's hide-away.

Wildwood, however, was lost in transition. Most of the people who had owned the family motels were well past retirement age, and new family members just did not have the interest, time or inclination to run the family motel business. In addition, like many farmers in their neighboring state of Pennsylvania, it was more profitable to sell to developers than to try to make a go of it at their advanced age. Who could blame them?

In addition, the 1980s had brought with them a different kind of a demand in the hospitality industry. Most vacationers with families were looking for something more than "one room plus a bath motel units." After all, it was the heyday of "suites," breakfast bars and all-encompassing resorts. People with families wanted two rooms, two TVs, two phones and a mini-kitchenette, all with a hot breakfast in the morning and a reasonable price tag. Enter the heyday of the "Suites Model" of hotel living.

Most of the small, albeit classic, motels in Wildwood just could not keep up with the demanding pace of the "new" benchmarks in hospitality. Wildwood and its space-age architecture was slowly becoming a distant memory.

One organization, that fastidiously documents the rapid pace of change in Wildwood, is The George F. Boyer Museum (The Wildwood Historical Society). They are there as the silent toll-takers of change. Like fans of a losing team who sat on the sidelines still cheering-on their heroes, even as they fell in defeat, they documented each demolition. They clipped every newspaper and magazine article, catalogued every negative, video and DVD, and saved every remnant of a forgotten brochure, tattered postcard or faded advertisement. They focused not only on the ephemeral but also on the brick and mortar from the island's rich history. Witness their rooms full of actual relics, be it bricks from The Shore Theater, tiles from the 1925 Sportland pool, bricks from the Blue Jay Motel, the date plaque from the 1927 boardwalk, bricks from local newspaper *The Wildwood Leader*, or other vestiges of long ago. And as the chief historians of the island, they are there to feed the rest of us, hungry for information, dates, names, places and documents. Their patience knows no boundaries and their knowledge of the "five-mile island" is without limits. They are indeed the true "keepers of the light."

In May of 2006, The National Trust for Historic Preservation placed Wildwood's Doo Wop motels as number one on its "Most Endangered" list. The national audience was sitting up and taking notice of this once-in-a-lifetime community of mid-20th century commercial resort architecture.

Man On A Mission:

Fedele Musso

Above:
Fedele Musso approaches neon bending from an artist's point- of -view. He is the perfect soldier in the war to save Wildwood's history of classic motel signage.

Right:
The Rio Motel sign lives in retirement in Golden Beach, Florida still shining on the Atlantic. The namesake motel was located at 4800 Ocean Ave. and Rio Grande when it met the wrecking ball in 2005.

Over the years, we have encountered many people who "rescue" vintage neon signs. They borrow trucks, cranes, and work crews (usually at some God-forsaken hour of the night or day), all in an effort to preserve a little piece of the past. They store their cache in warehouses, museums, empty stores, and even their own homes. They do all this as a way of saving a tiny part of our "collective history."

The mattresses were piled eight feet high as the great teardown ramped-up to breakneck pace in 2004. This photo, taken on October 20th of that year, shows this refuse pile in the front of the Bonanza Motel at Ocean Avenue and Stockton Road in Wildwood Crest. Look into the background of this photo and you will see two other victims awaiting their fate, the Hi Lili and the Kona Kai.

The drained pool and stripped façade of the Bonanza Motel share few clues to its once-magical past. The contrast is stark with the companion image of its heyday.

The Bonanza Motel, named for the hit television show of the 1960s, once was the home to family barbeques next to their glorious pool. Photo courtesy of ©Aladdin Color Inc. www.RetroStockPix.com

It is a funny thing about demolition. Like when a person you know loses weight, you forget what they looked liked when they were heavier. Same thing with buildings and signs; our minds seem to accept the new and forget the old; that is, until a photo or tangible piece of the past jogs our memory. Only then we realize what we have truly lost. That's why these people work against time to save anything they can, to remind us that we should appreciate the present before it becomes a piece of the past that has somehow slipped through our hands.

One man who had the foresight to save Wildwood's memories is Fedele (Fred) Musso, whose firm, Ultra Neon, began relighting South Florida in the early 1980s. A native of Scranton, Pennsylvania, whose family was prominent in the funeral business, Fedele vacationed in Wildwood as a child of the 1960s. In the 1970s, he owned a boardwalk business. The glitz of South Florida wooed him in the 1980s, but by the 1990s he was back, because "Florida had become over-regulated and congested," says Fedele.

Musso is a neon tube bender and sculptor with a deep appreciation for America's commercial heritage. Also, he has won, between 1992 and 2000, five electric sign design awards in five different cities in yearly competition sponsored by *Signs Of The Times Magazine*, a trade publication of the sign industry. When he returned to Wildwood in 1996, he started a program to collect Wildwood's abandoned neons. Volunteers were reluctant and his motives were ridiculed, but the signs trickled in.

"When development went haywire (from 2001-2006), the volume of neon to retrieve had become so overwhelming many were lost and space was at a premium," says Fedele. "There was no indication this was going to happen when I first returned. There was ample time to put some preservation in place, and locals just spun their wheels. Development can be a good thing, but the way it was done here was all wrong. Everything retail became bland vinyl condos."

Fred Musso was my guide in October of 2004 as we dashed from one teardown site to the next. This photo shows the wall of the Carousel Motel with a spray-painted sign that heralds its demise. The once-vibrant, carnival-like colors of the doors and roofline only hint at its past glory.

The Carousel Motel sign, hung from the building's front façade. Located at 5700 Ocean Ave. in Wildwood Crest, condominiums now rise from the rubble.

Fedele Musso tells story after story of getting there just "a minute too late" and coming upon an "iconic neon sign crushed into oblivion," unceremoniously dropped to the concrete below or lost to an indifferent scrap dealer.

The Carousel was once home to the royalty of the entertainment world, including Chubby Checker, Johnny Mathis and even Frank Sinatra. At the time it was built, it was Wildwood's largest motel. A sale of motel beds, carpets, tables and paintings is the collateral result in the final days before demolition.

Good spelling is a casualty of the quick teardown. The Earle Motel, located at 8700
Seaview Avenue in Wildwood Crest, was days from teardown in October of 2004.

A motel manager reflects his sadness at the closing of the Monte Cello Motel at 8400 Seaview Ave.
in Wildwood Crest. A smaller motel off the beach, like this one, was a ripe candidate for teardown.

The Notre Dame and Sunrise Motels in North Wildwood were
operated in tandem. They fell to the wrecker's ball the same way.

Carmen Aponte, an employee at the Notre Dame Motel in North Wildwood, expresses the collective sadness of Wildwood's darkest hours. She sees the furniture she cleaned and the beds she made unceremoniously sold at pennies on the dollar. 2201 Surf Ave.

From 2000 to 2005, 832 buildings were torn down in Wildwood and the districts of Wildwood, with many of those structures being motels. Fedele estimates that over 1000 neon signs were destroyed during this time. The years 2005 to 2007 recorded 249 demolition permits, and that number, thankfully, keeps going down.

In various neon graveyards, great visages of Wildwood's past sit side-by-side, upended, backwards and in reverse next to each other. It is a wrenching sight, to say the least. Up close, some are not truly recognizable. But erected and illuminated, as Fedele had done in the first Doo Wop Museum (1997-2004), their glory was evident.

Places that were once "friendly" competitors now sit, side-by-side, silently awaiting their final move. No longer are they the beaming, welcoming committee to Mom and Dads who had just made the argument-filled trip down from the city in an old car, *sans* air conditioning. No longer are they "an oasis in the desert" after the long walk home from the beach with burning feet, tired legs and exhausted, oil-covered bodies. No longer are they one of a group that stood, like soldiers, but would eventually fall, like dominos.

Now they sit in an empty lot or warehouse awaiting their next "assignment." For the unlucky, they are sitting in a dumpster next to cracked porcelain toilets and "magic finger" machines that have long-since been silenced and their digits immobilized. For others, they will find homes in the Doo Wop Museum across from The Wildwood Convention Center or in "good homes" as Fedele Musso likes to say, scattered like shimmering magic dust across the country. Homes like sign museums, collectors of Mid-century art, or just the kid (now middle-aged) who remembers the "luster" of a vacation in Wildwood and wants something to immortalize it.

Musso waxes nostalgic: "While it is easy to become disoriented as to what motel once stood where, many of the signs do live on. I continued to save them, even as the developers won. Several dozen were slated for the Doo Wop Museum, among them the well known Satellite and Ebb Tide Motels. Many others were acquired by Wildwood fanatics, neon sign collectors or artists," muses Musso.

Before the Doo Wop Museum opened its doors across from the Wildwood Convention Center, they had a humble home in this storefront on Pacific Avenue. Treasures salvaged as the wrecking ball swung were neatly placed along the walls and hung from the ceiling. Those like me, who had the privilege of a guided tour by Fred Musso, came away both a bit melancholy and motivated to get involved.

A 1950s-style kitchen, a treasure of the Doo Wop Preservation League.

PARKING FOR
3201 PACIFIC ONLY
ALL OTHERS TOWED
$10,000 FINE

Behind the museum's neat, yet humble interior, was the sign salvage yard. Fear not, the Bel Air Motel is still alive and well. They fly pretty much the same sign in a newer version. The salvage of this treasure is a worthy one.

Playpen Sign.

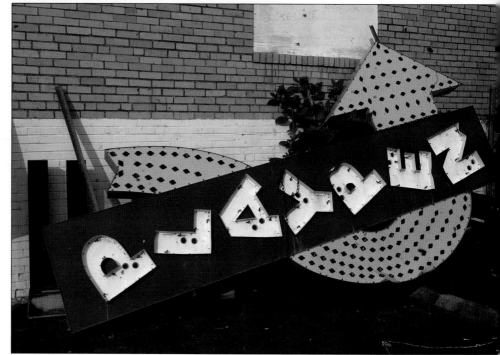

"One of the Rio Motel neons still overlooks the Atlantic Ocean, but from a residence in Golden Beach, Florida. The Blue Jay Motel and The Sans Souci Motel signs are in a residence in Lancaster, Pennsylvania. The old Ocean East Motel sign now glows over the Chesapeake Eastern Shore in a Maryland compound. The seven Bonanza neon letters went to five different owners, in four different states. A Thunderbird Motel neon is in upstate Vermont. Some Kona Kai Motel letters are in a pizza shop in Pottstown, Pennsylvania," Fred continues.

"Other signs are in Manhattan lofts, Palm Beach, or in the deep south in Dothan, Alabama. The biggest lot recently went to the National Save the Sign Museum in Minot, North Dakota, among them the flashing atoms Galaxie Motel, the Bolero Motel matador neon and the animated Sea Star Motel," Fred adds.

He sadly laments, "I really didn't want to let go of some of those signs, but it's time to move on. Space is hard to find, rent and taxes are high. I feel they all went to good homes; with interior applications those neon tubes will last forever."

However, Fedele is quick to add, "Neon again is under siege right now from the "Keep the Sky Dark" people, and this L.E.D. stuff I find extremely tacky. The medium of neon is just too peerless to ever go away. Most times when a client gets a neon piece from me they wonder how they ever lived so long without it."

Uncle Lou's parking. The boardwalk once boasted a series of restaurants that had familial names.

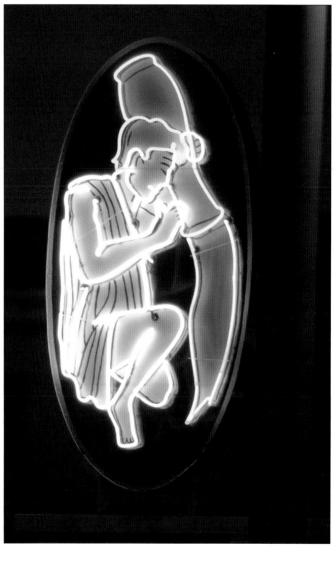

Though the Aquarius Motel still is open, this smaller delightful sign of Aquarius and his water jug vanished from the landscape. Shards of broken neon were left at the scene of this Wildwood mystery. Aquarius needs to return home from his Odyssey.

Sandy Court Apartments

Kona Kai motel sign, 7300 Ocean Ave., Wildwood Crest. The motel was demolished and the sign was sent to the four corners of the earth.

Hi Lili Motel, 7310 Ocean Ave., Wildwood Crest.
The motel is demolished, the sign's status unknown.

Condos For Sale on the site of the former Jay's Motel. Often regarded as the first motel in the Wildwoods, Jay's was a motorcourt-style complex built in 1952 by Lou and Will Morey. The condos have been completed and stand at the corner of Hildreth Avenue and Atlantic Avenue in Wildwood.

The irony did not escape me, as numerous bibles, a staple in bedside tables of the 1960s, flapped in the wind as places like the Tally Ho prepared to meet their maker. The Tally Ho was a sturdy little gem that had a great run. It was located on East Bennett Ave. in Wildwood.

Looking northwest from Morey's Pier, one can see the forever-changed face of Wildwood. Row after row, street after street of condominiums dot the landscape.

Neon Lights That Hypnotize:

Bob and Randy Hentges

Randy Hentges and his dad, Bob Hentges, of A.B.S. Sign Company are the foremost neon men in Wildwood. They stand under the Satellite Motel sign they created, which now resides in the sign garden at the Doo Wop Museum along Ocean Avenue near the Wildwood Convention Center.

Father and son sign legends, Bob and Randy Hentges, have been lighting the way in Wildwood for more than a half century. Their neon creations have withstood the test of time and become iconic symbols of simpler times and happier days, when vacationing was as easy as hopping in the car with Mom and Dad and throwing some suitcases in the trunk of a willow-green '66 Impala.

They created beautiful imagery that many would see as the "symbol" of all things Wildwood—signs that were sometimes more beautiful and intricate than the buildings they heralded. The signs had the ability to lure, dazzle, seduce and play, all simultaneously.

Bob and Randy Hentges were not the first sign builders in Wildwood, but as of this writing it is their signage that comprises most of what you now see there. Their business, A.B.S. Sign Company, has been creating neon (and other mediums) for more than fifty years. They did it when neon was the only medium used for signs, when neon dipped in popularity, and they make neon now, with the resurgence in this show-stopping art form.

Bob Hentges entered the sign business back in the early 1950s in a casual way. A kid he knew was working at a place, and they needed extra help so he recommended Bob Hentges. Two years later, when Bob's boss would not raise his pay to $1 an hour, he went to work for another sign company. He stayed with ACE Signs for eight years, then decided to branch out on his own. That same year he was elected mayor (the youngest at 26 years old) of West Wildwood, New Jersey. With a borrowed wad of cash ($2500), an old utility truck, and some sheet metal tools, Bob started his own business. From an inauspicious beginning, one of the most prominent sign companies in the Northeast grew to become an industry leader: A.B.S. Sign Company (Always Better Service).

Bob Hentges reminisces about all the sign companies that helped to put Wildwood on the map. "Beginning with the middle '50s, there was Allied Sign Company, owned by Ted Polis, (now deceased). Later, The Lanza Sign Company was established around 1970. Ted Polis sold Allied Sign Company to Harry Lanza and it became known as the Allied Lanza Sign Company. Harry Lanza passed away and his sign company was taken over by a company called JT Sign Company, from Vineland. The owner of JT Sign Company also passed away, and his widow sold it to another gentlemen. Allied Lanza is now out of business."

Bob continues to weave his tale, "Then there was Casimer Szczur. He used to work for the original Allied Sign Company, but left that company in 1955, and started Ace Sign Company. Mr. Szczur died in the 1980s. In 1965, I bought out Ace Sign Company and retired that name."

Pondering, Bob continues, "There was also a Wildwood sign company called Seashore Sign Company, started by a man named Jim Lou. He sold that company several years ago. Seashore manufactured mostly wood and painted signs. However, before he sold the company, he did do some very nice electrical signs."

Bob adds, "There was also another sign company called Protesto Sign Company, located on 17th Street in North Wildwood. Mr. Protesto moved to Route 47 in Dennis Township. He did some electrical signs, and about 10 years ago my son, Randy, bought Protesto Sign Company and retired that name."

Bob gives a special "tip of the hat" to sign designers and painters Jack Driscoll and Albert Eichhorn. "Both," according to Bob, "were masters in their field."

Summing it all up, he adds, "Accordingly, the four original signs companies were Allied Sign Company, Ace Sign Company, A.B.S Sign Company and Allied Lanza Sign Company. The other names 'came and went' over the years, and A.B.S Sign Company is the only remaining original sign company still located in Wildwood since February, 1964," said Bob with a mixture of pride and lament.

"During the 1950s and 1960s, a lot of the rooming houses in town came down and the motel building craze was going full speed ahead," says Bob. "A lot of these motel owners hadn't even thought of a name for their place, but they needed a sign. So we did it all: we named the motel, built and installed the sign, and ended up creating a logo for their business that they would give to a printer to put on everything from brochures to ashtrays."

By the late 1970s, most of the signs that were erected in town had been built by four different sign companies. As the decades progressed, A.B.S. Sign Company would eventually take pride in knowing that their signs made up most of the signs that remained. The 1970s and 1980s were dry years for neon. Plastic signs were all the rage. Neon was too expensive and too fragile; repairs were too costly. However, by the end of the 1980s, everyone would agree that nothing beat neon for the variety of colors, designs and applications, not to mention how memorable it was to the customers. As Bob says, "If you can dream it, you can make it with neon."

Bob, now 72 years old, attributes most of their success in the business to their innovative designers and the skill of his son. "I remember Randy came to me in the early 1980s and said he wanted to go to a school in West Palm Beach that taught neon tube-bending. Now he had been working after school and on Saturdays in the business. However, when our neon glass blower retired, Randy asked me if maybe he should learn the glass-blowing business. So, he wanted to go to Florida for one week. He ended up staying for two and costing me the best $2500 I ever invested in my life. It all came together for Randy in Florida."

With the 1990s in full swing, Randy pretty much assumed most of the business. Dad still had his "other job" as a surrogate court judge of Cape May County, now 37 years and counting. Randy and his crew spent a lot of time creating new neon (and other sign formats), servicing existing neon, and dreaming of "the next phase," when Wildwood would be rediscovered.

With "rediscovery" came innovative places like The Starlux Hotel and Coastal Broadcasting, both of which sought Randy's expertise, not only in sign design but also in façade structure. The Starlux was a new hotel (built on the framework of an existing motel) created as an homage to Googie architecture. Coastal Broadcasting wanted a classic look, a throw back to radio stations of the 1930s and 1940s. A.B.S. Sign Company created a streamlined Art Deco look for their building, not only in the signage but in the metal façade and wrapped neon borders as well.

"I think the end of the teardown is here. There is a huge glut of condominiums in this town that are not turning over as quickly as the developers had hoped. We're starting to see an upswing in the desire to "return to neon," not only by this community but by many others that we service," remarks Randy, "We've also been approached by national businesses."

A.J. Figueroa of A.B.S. Sign Company appears to be single-handedly supporting the new Bristol Plaza sign that is being hung by Randy Hentges and his team.

A.B.S. Sign Company gives a rare summer performance as they hang The Bristol Plaza sign during high season. A.B.S. Sign Company proves that the melding of the best of the old and new technology, can be seamless when done right. 6407 Ocean Ave., Wildwood Crest, N.J.

The old Bristol sign is retired to the back lot at A.B.S. Sign Company.

In early July 2009, Randy and his crew erected a new sign at The Bristol Motel. In the course of one day, they removed the old sign and erected the new neon one, all as a crowd of hundreds watched from balconies and sidewalks surrounding the ocean-front motel. Their three trucks, all wrapped in photos of their past triumphs, strategically weaved the sign between the hotel's façade and the high-tension wires strung along the street. As the sun set in the west, the new Bristol sign joined its siblings on the strip and glowed in unison with them along Ocean Avenue. The crowd began tossing out compliments about Wildwood's latest neon dream.

To drive up and down the roads of this coastal gem with Randy and marvel at what "is left" of the great signs, one has to take a deep breath. Randy muses on the legacy that he and he father created: "You know, you're so busy building the signs, getting them up, making sure they work properly, making sure the customer is happy, and getting them billed, that you rarely have the time to step away and look at the whole picture." Well, if Randy and Bob did take that moment and step away, they would soon realize that most of "our" collective memory of what is, what has been, and probably what is to come in Wildwood, New Jersey, came out of their shop. Moreover, isn't that something that all of us strive for in our careers? To create something so beautiful and everlasting that those who come after us will savor and appreciate our hard work for years to come.

The Suitcase Motel is located at 1500 New Jersey Ave. in North Wildwood. When the original owner was stymied for a name for her new venture, Bob Hentges jumped in with this whimsical one. A man and woman reside in a neon-encrusted suitcase high above the parking lot.

"The Cone Man" once welcomed guests to the Hudson Family Restaurant, which was at 5901 Atlantic Ave. I invited him home to sit upon my roof but he wisely stayed in Wildwood.

Pyramid Motel, Atlantic Ave. & St. Paul Ave., Wildwood Crest.

Sea Ray Motel, 5006 Ocean Ave., Wildwood.

Sahara Motel, 510 E. 18th Ave., North Wildwood.

Sea Gull Motel, Cresse & Atlantic Ave., Wildwood.

Surf Haven Motel, 1601 Surf Ave., North Wildwood.

Sea Scape Inn, 400 E. Crocus Rd., Wildwood Crest.

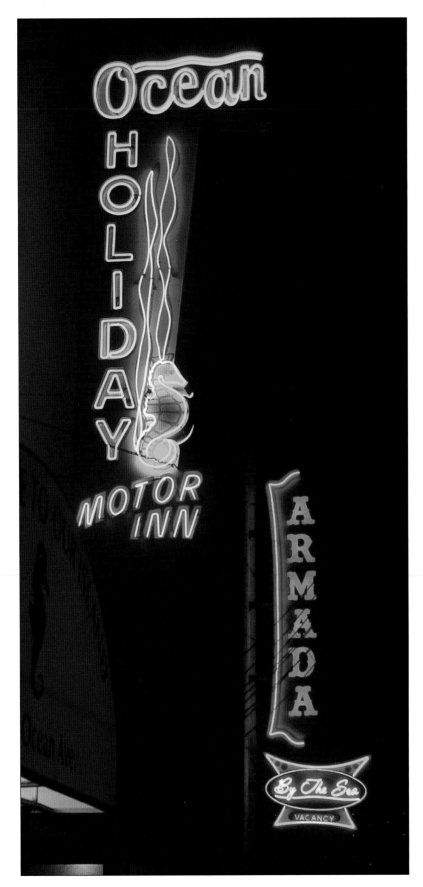

Ocean Holiday and the Armada By-the-Sea, located at 6501 & 6503 Ocean Avenue in the Crest. Ocean Avenue is the closest Wildwood has to the Vegas strip. At night, convertibles cruise up and down, checking out the motel's nightlife.

Bonito Motel, 236 Spicer Ave, Wildwood. A distinctively beautiful sign either in daylight or in evening's glow.

Bonito

Twilight Motel, 210 E. Spicer Ave., Wildwood. The Caribbean color scheme makes you want to put on tie-dye and listen to Bob Marley.

Mango Motel, 209 E. Spicer Ave., Wildwood. The Mango is the neighbor of the Twilight and they both could be props in a detective "film noir" movie set in the Florida Keys.

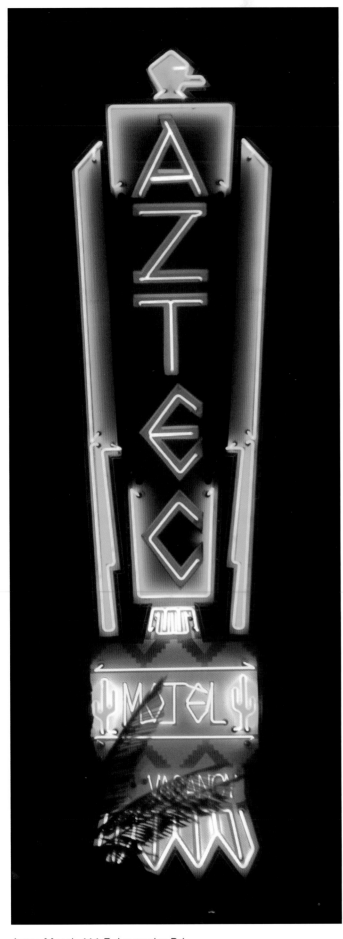

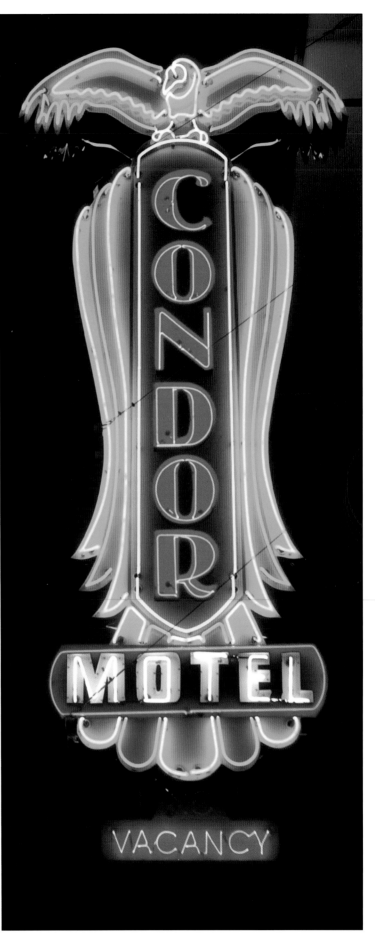

Aztec Motel, 411 E. Lavender Rd.,
Wildwood Crest.

Condor Motel, 16th & Ocean Ave., North Wildwood.

Cape Cod Inn Motel, 6110 Atlantic Avenue, Wildwood Crest. A lighthouse stands central in this rotating giant that tries to out-do the Pan Am ball up the street.

Pan American Hotel, 5901Ocean Ave. at Crocus, Wildwood Crest. When is the World's Fair coming to town? This beauty was originally created by Harry Lanza of Allied Lanza Sign Company and hung with the able assistance of his son Wayne Lanza. In the last ten years, Randy Hentges of A.B.S. Sign Company rebuilt the ball to the original specifications with more climate friendly components.

Ala Kai Resort Motel, 8301 Atlantic Ave., Wildwood Crest. Hula girls and golden yellow neon whisper to the weary traveler to stop in and stay awhile.

American Safari Motel, 5610 Ocean Ave., Wildwood Crest. An award-winning newer sign that says this place is an adventure.

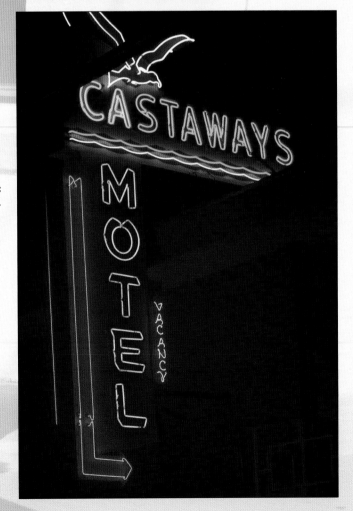

Castaways Motel, 3700 Atlantic Ave., Wildwood.

Monaco Motel, 4211 Ocean Ave., Wildwood. When this baby was built, actress Grace Kelly was the new princess of Monaco. Staying here made you feel like royalty, but so did the Imperial and the Kings Inn.

Florentine Family Motel, 1901 Surf Ave., North Wildwood.

Caprice Motel, 4200 Ocean Ave.,
Wildwood.

Bird Of Paradise Motel, 333 East 26th
Street, North Wildwood.

Coliseum Ocean Resort, 416 East Miami Ave., Wildwood Crest.

Isle of Palms, 3200 Atlantic Ave., Wildwood.

Jolly Roger Motel, 6805 Atlantic Avenue, Wildwood Crest. A great wall sign that directs travelers to the next great Doo Wop masterpiece in the Wildwoods.

Building the Future Out of the Past:

Richard Stokes

Richard Stokes seamlessly blended the past and present with his rethinking of the Shalimar Motel in Wildwood Crest. He saved the best elements, played off their strengths and created a Shalimar that competes with the amenities found in new construction. 6405 Atlantic to Ocean Ave at Rosemary Rd., Wildwood Crest.

The StarLux sign created by Randy Hentges.

45-year-old Richard Stokes, an architectural *wunderkid* and native of Cleveland, Ohio, landed in Philadelphia in 1990. He is one of those gifted people who always seems to have an 'intuitive understanding' of the situation. Although he did not discover Wildwood until 1999 (he by-passed it "on the way to Cape May"), once there, his life would be forever changed. "I heard about Wildwood through Steve Izenour. Steve told me all about it and when I finally went, I could not believe I had literally 'passed it by' all of those years! Nevertheless, when I saw it, I saw it with 'fresh eyes,' not jaded by any sentimental attachments to the place," explains Richard.

As a colleague of famed architect, Steve Izenour, (both worked together at Venturi, Scott Brown and Associates) Richard learned much about "Commercial Modernism" through Steve's dealings with the iconic town. Commercial Modernism was only a generic term for Wildwood's architecture; other names were Googie (mainly in California), MiMo (from Miami) and Populuxe. Richard adds, "Wildwood really is a unique place, not just the buildings and the signs, but the concentration of all of them on one strip (Ocean Avenue). What is unusual about the strip was the way it was developed. It is on beach land, block to block, onto the beach and only single-use motels (no gas stations, car washes, restaurants, etc.). At night, to drive down that street was a heady experience," says Stokes.

Richard considers the years 1999 to 2009 pivotal in Wildwood's lifespan. "In 1999, Wildwood was still in its original and pristine state. It was still 'dipped in Amber'," explains Richard. "They still had signs that said 'Color TV's & telephones in every room' and even 'sunken living rooms' at one place (The Tuscany)! Development bypassed Wildwood until that year. Wildwood had a stigma that developers could not get past. Then Steve Izenour invited the design studios of University of Pennsylvania, Kent State and Yale to spend time and work in Wildwood. Design studios are part of an architectural curriculum, that allows for 'in the field' work. That was a turning point for Wildwood," says Richard.

Richard elaborates, "The studies that Steve Izenour did on Wildwood turned things around very quickly. Suddenly, everyone was saying to one another, 'this place isn't so bad!' It has beautiful beaches, a great boardwalk and these great little motels!

Steve's study had a huge effect on tourism, and part of that surprisingly would prove to be a negative. Value in the land was now noted and small mo-

tels were starting to be replaced by condominiums, very swiftly. Moreover, the momentum continued to build at break-neck speed. Wildwood was lucky the recession kicked in. It certainly slowed things down quite a bit," says Stokes.

Richard, with a sigh, continues, "However, within that brief amount of time, the landscape had totally changed. It was almost unrecognizable. It started to look like any other place on the Jersey shore (beach-to-bay condominiums) and that was a major negative. We had fought to save those motels, but a lot of money was involved. In addition, many of those buildings were functionally obsolete. A motel had to be in a special category to be suitable for renovation. The Shalimar, with its high-end Doo Wop style, had it. The Wingate (now The Starlux) was generic, so we had to 'invent' a style for that," says Richard with pride.

Richard continues to explain how preservationists fought against money, time, functionality and politics. "Most of the older motels in Wildwood were built during a time when things were done on the cheap. We would have to go in and replace entire HVAC (heating/air conditioning) systems. That is why so many of these motels did not lend themselves to renovation. With The Starlux (owned by The Morey Organization), we were able to combine rooms, add a floor, and add elevators and a lounge. It was a large investment to renovate The Wingate into The Starlux. That is why so few can do it," explains Richard.

The Wingate Motel provided the bones for the Starlux. Notice the owner's home on premises, the lack of a pool and only three floors. Photo courtesy of Aladdin Color Inc. www.RetroStockPix.com

An inspired sketch of the StarLux, by architect Richard Stokes. Note the large oval windows on the addition that never made it to the final renovation. Courtesy of Richard Stokes, Stokes Architecture, Philadelphia, Pa.

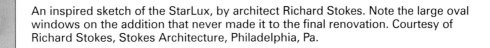

The StarLux is the first major hotel you see as you enter Wildwood via Rio Grande Avenue from off the island. The past lies on the present, in a loving tribute to mid-century architecture.

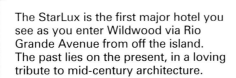

A simple brochure rack has a playful air, which prods guests to play scrabble with the letters. The Astro Lounge of the StarLux Hotel.

Lava lamps and glass beads provide a groovy vibe for the framing device created by the windows in the Astro Lounge at the StarLux.

Ashley Bulboff , age 11, and her brother John Bulboff, age13, of Pittsgrove, New Jersey enjoy the hot tub at the StarLux.

But to anyone who has ever stayed at The Starlux, the results of Jack Morey's vision and Richard Stokes's design skills (did I mention Randy Hentges's sign?) are dazzling and time-warping. There is a reminiscent quality when staying there, of Disneyworld and its Prime Time Café. The Prime Time Café is a recreation of a 1950s family kitchen, replete with a plastic-laminate table and vinyl-padded chairs, knick-knacks, the food of the time-period (lots of meatloaf and mashed potatoes), and of course an apron-wearing "mom" to serve you. Well, staying at The Starlux has that same "traveling through time" feeling. You are enveloped in the beauty, simplicity and imagination of the 1950s, only with the finest of present-day amenities. From the boomerang coffee tables and bubble lights, to the boldly colored bedding schemes, it is a vacation one needs to experience if you want to turn back the hands of the time.

Just like The Starlux's former self, The Wingate, when the Doo Wop motels of Wildwood are critically examined, a series of patterns begins to emerge. Richard explains it in this way: "In all of Wildwood, I think there were three room plans total. Most of the motels had the same layout and construction style. What gave each property its physical 'uniqueness' (customer service aside) were three things: (1) their sign (proclaiming the theme), (2) the façade treatment (then carried out to the rooms), and (3) the office/check-in/owner's quarters."

Stokes continues, "On Ocean Avenue, most of the motels originally were all about the same. Then a sign company comes in, comes up with a name and the façade treatment follows it. For example, the Tiki-style

The greatest single loss to the Wildwood Doo Wop movement was the Satellite Motel. A strong and persistent campaign to save this mid-century masterpiece failed. Unique among Wildwood's motels with its triangular windows, its southwestern paint scheme and that space-age lobby; this is the one that got away. Located at 5900 Atlantic Ave. at Aster Rd. in Wildwood Crest. Courtesy of © Aladdin Color Inc. wwwRetroStockPix.com

motels are all integrated units with the 'A' frames added over each one to give it a distinct look. Of course, some were different. On the beach, there is The Singapore. It was the most elaborate in design. I always remember the name of its restaurant, the 'Bamboo Noshery' (now Sharkey's Grill). It's quite the place."

Naturally, with the successes of places like The Starlux and The Shalimar came great losses as well. "The greatest loss (of the motels) in Wildwood was The Satellite. Out of all of the motels, it was the most high-style. It had a beautiful owner's suite and public spaces. It was like a giant California Ranch House, over-scaled with its triangular windows. It was small, but could have made a great boutique motel. The owner sold it to a developer for millions. It would have been quite expensive to do a renovation on it. The entire infrastructure had to be replaced. It would have been difficult to expand because of the parking situation. Parking is a prime motivator in renovations. You start with the number of cars and then work your way back to motel units. Unlike the Surfside Diner, where the owner gave it to us and we disassembled it and reassembled it in another spot, The Satellite would not have worked like that. It was concrete block walls with a wooden frame. It could not be moved easily," says Richard.

"The Wildwood Diner was a big loss too, in the restaurant category. It was destroyed for a high rise that never came to be; now it is just an empty lot," adds Richard. The blue-green paneled diner was a 1958 Superior Diner; in fact, it was the only one of its kind in existence. When it was delivered, the owner simply had the original stainless steel one pushed to the back of the lot behind it.

The vertigo-inducing facade of the Ebb Tide Motel made this another hard demolition to swallow. One of Wildwood's first DooWop motels and certainly its first with a wicked sense of humor. Designed by Lou Morey in 1957 and located at 5711 Atlantic Avenue in the Crest until its 2003 teardown. Courtesy of © Aladdin Color Inc. wwwRetroStockPix.com

Wildwood Diner Sign

This is sadness times two for me, since diners represent my awakening to preservation lost, and Wildwood is a natural fit for a classic diner. This photo, taken in 1995, shows a green-paneled, 1958 Superior diner that was one-of–a-kind. The lot at Spencer & Atlantic Avenues stands vacant until this day.

For every person who reveled in Wildwood's past, the demolition years continue to be an open wound in his or her soul's memory. "The demolition could have been halted," explains Richard. "The city gave out the permits. Without permits, these people could not build (or tear down) a thing. You need a historic commission in place to regulate such things. At the time, old-school politicians ran Wildwood Crest. They were not behind the Doo Wop movement at all. They had seen these buildings day after day, year after year and viewed them as dumps. Moreover, the new condominiums meant higher tax revenues. They saw these old buildings as disposable. They needed to see it with 'fresh eyes.' There is now a new administration in Wildwood Crest that is supportive of their recent past. In addition, Wildwood Mayor Ernie Troiano has been supportive of moving the city forward and preserving the historic district. The city helped pay for the Doo Wop Museum's Surfside project," says Richard happily.

Which projects (motels) would be suitable for new expansion or renovation? "Expansion of The Caribbean would be very feasible. With its spiral ramp, it's a real beauty," says Richard. "Then there is the Attaché; it has a great location and great potential. It could be combined with The Gondolier. Not to be forgotten is The Jolly Roger, which has a great plan with the courtyard, and pool opening out to the ocean view. I have already renovated some of the rooms," says Richard with obvious excitement. "We need more guys like (builder) Jack Morey to move Wildwood into the future. Jack is a 'big picture' guy. He travels a lot. He knows what is going on outside of Wildwood and brings it home."

Richard is inspired by hotels in other parts of the country, as well as Wildwood. "My favorite motels/ hotels (outside of Wildwood)? Probably in Miami Beach—the Eden Roc and Fountainebleu. In addition, Palm Springs has a nice section of classic motels. I recall The Orbit In (sic) in specific as being very interesting. But in Wildwood (aside from The Starlux and The Shalimar), it would be The Caribbean."

The Astro Lounge at the StarLux seems like the coolest living room this side of Palm Springs.

Some say, like all fabulous futuristic designs, the seminal moment for Wildwood could have been the 1939 World's Fair. Richard ponders this, "Well, (Morris) Lapidus designed the Fountainebleu and the Sheraton BAL Harbor (formerly the Americana) in Miami. The Pan American in Wildwood was inspired by the The Americana (now destroyed). The rotating ball at top was an homage to the 1964 World's Fair. I would say it started at the '39 World's Fair, went through Miami Beach and then to Wildwood. As well, we cannot forget that the boardwalk tram cars came directly from The 1939 World's Fair! Yes, I can definitely see that. Commercial Modernism was a forward thinking style. That was the essence of the 1939 World's Fair."

Eight trams in all were brought (in 1949) from the 1939 World's Fair to the wooden decks of the Wildwood Boardwalk. While some are beginning to be replaced (for better tires, tougher suspensions, etc.,), the lion's share are still the original cars that Sebastian Ramagosa (a Wildwood visionary) brokered from that future-altering event.

Richard believes that Wildwood has turned a corner. The demolition has all but stopped (or at least slowed down to a snail's pace). Preservationists have a better footing (backed by new zoning laws) moving developers forward with guidance and structure. In addition, the visionaries who have always loved Wildwood are bringing great things back for her future.

The Jolly Roger Motel has all the correct building blocks for a renaissance of cosmic proportions. It is a stunner as is, but with a little T.L.C., it is off the charts. The pool looks across Ocean Ave. to the Atlantic Ocean.

The Wildwood Sign at the Boardwalk and Rio Grande Avenue is both simple and incredibly sophisticated at the same time. The cast beach balls and the bigger- than-life letters provide a family with a venue for a snapshot that defines them for a generation. Parades of families organize their ranks for the click of the shutter before the Wildwood Sign, possibly rivaling only those taken at the pyramids of Egypt or the Coliseum in Rome. Richard Stokes hit it out of the park.

Richard comments on what he hopes the future of Wildwood will look like: "I hope not to see the high-rises. I like the scale of Wildwood. It is an urban scale, but not a dense urban scale. Center city Wildwood can support more mid-rise (ten- to twelve-story) structures, not a twenty-five-story property. That would not be appropriate. It destroys the look of the place. I would like to see further enhancement of the boardwalk and the beaches. We are currently looking at how to utilize sections of the beach as they do in Santa Cruz, California. We want to make it more accessible to pedestrians. Now it is just an auto destination. I (along with many others) would like to create a park on the landward side of the beach, with a bike path, connecting existing ones in North Wildwood and Wildwood Crest. Right now, all of this land on this immensely large beach is mostly unused. We can draw more people to the beach by making it more inviting. I think it is worth reassessing," says Richard glowingly.

If You Build It, They Will Come:

Jack Morey

Mariner's Landing Pier is all aglow in the setting sun of a summer's night and the neon wrapping the Balloon Race and the Giant Wheel.

Years ago, while assisting my husband with his previous book, *Hometown Diners*, we had the opportunity to learn some enlightening things about the preservation of "places of historical significance" that were still operational. As much as all of us never wanted to see a diner closed, and marveled at them for their intrinsic beauty, their "captured in time" look and the other elements that made these "pieces of history" come to life, we neglected the obvious.

The fact remained that we were not visiting these places in The Smithsonian Institution. They were real, operating businesses - with the same problems as other real, operating businesses, regardless of the fact that they were "little stainless steel time capsules - relics of our not-too-distant past." In addition, usually their owners were so busy making a living that the whole "diner mystique" was completely lost on them. *They* were the true "insiders" of the industry, not the "voyeurs", like the rest of us – devotees who paid homage and studied the industry from conventions, books and niche publications. As they say in the diner world, "you cannot eat history."

When you work day to day in the trenches, the allure that everyone else sees can sometimes elude you. You cannot comprehend the "movement" that has built up around your (take your choice here) motel, diner, business, etc., until you fully step away from it. The fact that your piece of the world has become an "emotional landmark" for so may others is often not completely visible through eyes blurred by the sweat of hard work.

Forty-eight year old Jack Morey is rugged, charismatic, humble, and heir to the dynasty that built much of what the rest of us have come to know as Wildwood.

His brother Will and he are the sons of Will and Jackeye Morey. Will, Sr. was part of the 1950s dynamic 'brotherhood' of Ray, Lou, Bill and Charlie Morey. While all were involved in the building trade to some degree, it was Will and Lou (both, sadly, now deceased) that would break out as the leaders in shaping much of the landscape in Wildwood. Although they did not refer to it as Doo Wop back then, eventually the Googie architecture that our California friends have learned to appreciate would come to rest on the shores of Wildwood, and be known by the mid-1990s as Doo Wop (an homage to Philadelphia sound of the 1950s).

Will (Wilbert) and Bill (and their wives) spent much of the off-season in Florida. So much time in fact, that young Jack and Will would eventually graduate from a prep school in Fort Lauderdale, Florida. While in Florida, Wilbert would accumulate ideas that the brothers would later bring back to their summer resort hometown of Wildwood and attempt to "adapt them." They referred to this technique as 'Wildwoodize,' resulting in much of the Floridian feel one would experience when in Wildwood, including the abundance of "Flagler (one of Florida's

great developers), Yellow" and "Palm Beach Pink" color schemes. Florida also 'willed' Wildwood motel names like Eden Roc, Sans Souci and The Diplomat.

It would eventually be Will's sons, Jack and Will, who picked up the ball and carried it on behalf of their famous father. "At times I'm a bit of a frustrated architect," says Jack. "I saw Wildwood as a one of a kind, internationally acclaimed resort town opportunity. We had this wonderful collection of unique Mid Century architectural motels, a one of a kind boardwalk and one of the widest and most beautiful beaches in the world."

Jack marveled at what he saw in Wildwood. "I kept looking at it as what was needed to create one of the world's best and most memorable seaside towns that was a true celebration of Americana and the classic American family," elaborates Jack. "Early on, I learned that for this vision to be successful it would take an abundance of entrepreneurs, not museum curators. In other words, this could not be successful by being a subsidized museum project, but rather had to deliver real entertainment goods and services to hard working tourists that had a wide array of competing options. In short, it had to make money or it would die."

Jack told *The Philadelphia Inquirer* in May of 2006, "It's a huge frustration that nationally people recognize the architectural importance of Wildwood, but locally it continues to be disregarded as the buildings continue to be torn down."

Jack intuitively understood that it would eventually be a blending of the old with the new that would bring success to his beloved seaside community. "What you need to do is to take those preservationist ideas and reinvent them. If you think about it, our neighbor to the south, Cape May, is not really 'preserved' as much as it is reinvented. Preservation is a tool with a wide definition that can be used in the private sector. Individual entrepreneurs compete with one another. Competition is good for everyone. When Wildwood was built, it was not built with preservation or design controls in place."

Jack became the first president of the Doo Wop Preservation League in 1996. He continues to explain the perfect amalgam between the past and the future, from a planning perspective, "One of our goals was not only to create an historic district, but to also attract new entrepreneurs to create "new" or "retro" 1950s and 1960s institutions. Wildwood has a different beach, boardwalk and collection of hotels than any other seaside community."

However, he also lamented great losses like The Golden Nugget amusement attraction on old Hunt's Pier, just like the rest of her fans. Yet, at the same time, he was greatly heartened by the success of the Doo Wop Preservation League's "saving the Surfside Diner" and turning it into their showplace museum and sign garden.

Jack Morey overlooks the Morey's legacy as he rides the Giant Wheel, but Jack is always grounded in his love of people and the town his family helped define. Along with his brother Will, the Morey's Organization has invested in the bright future of Wildwood. If you build it, they will come.

The corkscrewing Sea Serpent coaster on Mariner's Landing Pier.

Enough lights? At Morey's Piers, the rides may change
every few years but the fun and adventure is constant.

Jack Morey thanks a young guest for her patience in waiting for the Giant Wheel to take her for her ride in the sky. Jack has his offices looking out on the amusement pier.

The Skyride takes guests high above Adventure Pier and gives them a breath taking view of the boardwalk below. I liked it so much I have one at home.

Mariner's Landing Pier.

The Blue Palms Motel, at 3601 Atlantic Avenue, has a bird's-eye view of the Giant Wheel on Morey's Piers. Located in the heart of the downtown, kids anxious to get to the boardwalk don't have far to go.

Jacek Bartha, of the Pan American Hotel staff, proudly shows off the signature ball that rotates on the roof. Originally designed and built by sign maker extraordinaire Harry Lanza of Allied Lanza Sign Company, it was rebuilt to specs by Randy Hentges of A.B.S. Sign Company in recent years.

The Morey's Organization brand is on many of Wildwood's most treasured landmarks. It employs over 1,600 college students a year from over 30 different countries. Morey's Piers include Mariner's Landing Pier, Surfside Pier, Adventure Pier, Raging Waters Waterpark, and the Ocean Oasis Waterpark & Beach Club. Overnight accommodations include The Starlux Hotel, The Pan America Hotel, The Port Royal Hotel, The Jolly Roger Motel, The Blue Palms Motel and Seapointe Village Condominiums.

Even with the litany of amusement parks and hotels that he and his family have built, it is the public spaces of Wildwood which make him smile. "I am very proud of the Wildwood sign (the giant retro sign at the end of the Rio Grande Gateway on the beach, surrounded by oversized beach balls, designed by Richard Stokes). It is a 'stake in the ground.' A powerful statement. When you build something in a public space, people are forced to notice it. It is the most photographed item when visitors take the tour of Wildwood. It creates a lasting memory."

Jack sees the future of Wildwood in a direct and succinct way, "Worse case scenario: make Wildwood proud of its elite tackiness."

We chatted about the "Disney visit", when a team from Walt Disney World came to town in the early 1990s looking to "recreate" a boardwalk theme. "You want the honest answer?" says Jack. "We were working with renowned architect Steve Izenour and Disney was one of his clients. When they decided to do this 'Boardwalk' theme, he suggested to them that they come to Wildwood to see 'the real thing.'"

The "maintaining the old, and incorporating the new theme" arises again with Jack when we continue to discuss the famous Wildwood Boardwalk. "It's constantly changing," says Jack. "Old and pretty is great, but what makes a boardwalk really powerful is what's new. Do I wish it was cleaner, better, had more hotels and restaurants on it? Absolutely. But being 'gritty' is not necessarily a bad thing. But I would like it a little less gritty," Jack says with a wry smile.

Years ago, with the help of Steve Izenour, the Morey Organization stopped positioning themselves as a "theme park" and embraced their true gifts. In fact, their mission statement says it quite succinctly: "To provide a spectacular family recreational experience in an exceptionally safe, clean, friendly and unique environment." Jack smiles when he hears those words and is quick to add, "My brother and I fought over the wording of that for weeks."

Everyone you speak to in Wildwood has high praise for Jack and Will Morey and the entire Morey Organization. Many in Wildwood believe, it was people like the Moreys whose dedication to Wildwood eventually pulled it out of the challenging times of the mid 1980s and saw it through to the present.

The glorious pool at the Pan American Hotel has a fine view of the Atlantic and the finest collection of Jersey Palm Trees around. 5901 Ocean Ave., Wildwood Crest.

Whether it was a new rollercoaster, waterpark or 'retro' hotel, they were doing everything they could to keep Wildwood on the map.

The introduction of a new hotel built on the framework of an existing one was a fascinating concept. Many of the mid-century motels in Wildwood had proven themselves unsuitable for renovation. When the Moreys decided to renovate an existing L-shaped unit, two blocks from the ocean on Rio Grande Avenue, the world stood up and took notice. They commissioned acclaimed architect Richard Stokes to renovate the former Wingate Motel into a lavish, doo-wopped theme 'retro' experiential hotel. The result was nothing less than awe-inspiring. The Starlux stood as a testament to the world that you can take the old, renovate it to please the modern traveler (both in accommodations and visually), yet still maintain the look and feel of a vintage hotel without any of the drawbacks of a 60 year old property. The Starlux is just the beginning in the Wildwood universe of possibilities.

With a group of vintage motels/hotels under their flag, the Morey's Organization has developed a system to bring out the best in each of them. "We have relationships with a 'collection' of designers we go to depending on the project. We have a new 'interior' group called 3 North out of Richmond, Virginia, which specializes in small boutique hotels, not brands or national franchises," says Jack.

"There was a time when we 'doo-wopped' everything," continues Jack. "Eventually we realized that the story of these motels and hotels was much richer than that. We learned that if you do not have a franchise name, you have to have a story. We look at the I. Q. of a property - its intangible qualities. Moreover, we discovered that it was about the people. It is not about what's 'hot and new' anymore, it is about what is 'special and timeless.' That is people. That is families."

One hotel that he has a special interest in is The Port Royal. "My dad had a partner. His name was Mr. Palmer Way. He liked math, so he went to Princeton," says Jack. "He studied under Einstein - the Einstein. Then Mr. Way went to Harvard for his law degree. He and my dad were partners. My dad flunked out of high school, twice, and never attended college. Yet he and Palmer had a similar vision. Pretty interesting."

Jack continues, "We are now partners with his sons, John and Marty. John operates the Port Royal. Their grandfather Martin (Palmer's dad) was the county judge and loved boats. He owned a 75-foot sailing schooner that he purchased from the Coast Guard during prohibition called 'The Wayfarer.' Eventually it sank, many years ago, off the British Virgin Islands. But it is all a part of the Port Royal mystique."

Jack concedes that family is a huge part of why he does what he does. He works not only for the sake of his father and mother before him, or for his wife Karen, and their two sons, Jordon and Zack. Or for his brother Will, his wife Janice and their two boys Kyle and Will, Jr., but for *all* of the families who come to vacation in this seaside resort with a one-of-a kind boardwalk, Mid Century motels, a world class beach and some of the most award-winning amusement and waterparks in the country !

When asked what he would like his legacy to be, Jack is quick to answer, "I am not interested in legacies. I just want to be a good dad and husband and do a little inventive building on the side. When work stops being work, and starts being an interesting hobby, that is when the momentum rolls. It is about trying to build something special for people to enjoy. My Dad started this business without even a feasibility study. Had he had one, he probably never would have moved off of square one," says Jack smiling.

Don't Take My Kodachrome Away:

David & Eric Bard

24th Street Motel, 2401 Surf Ave., Wildwood. Demolished in 2006. Courtesy of ©Aladdin Color Inc. www.RetroStockPix.com

Recently, when we cleaned out my parents' home, readying it for sale, I came across stacks and stacks of brochures and postcards from distant vacation resorts. When I was a very young child, we would take a yearly, weeklong vacation.

During those years, I remember my mother placing calls (and writing notes) to chambers of commerce in these little towns (usually New England and the Pocono's) with the expectation of receiving 'a package' from them. The 'package' usually consisted of a cover letter on thick, linen stock (usually written in beautiful handwriting), a lovely brochure and the ever-popular postcard. I remember 'studying' the postcards for what seemed like hours. I examined the lake, taking special note of the smiles on the sunbather's faces. I memorized every detail of the guest room, noting with curious wonder the knotty-pine paneling (I had no idea what knotty-pine paneling was at the time). The point is that my mother would make our vacation decision based solely on the postcards and brochures sent to her. So would everyone else during the 1960s and early 1970s, resulting in the power of that almost forgotten medium.

David Bard had a thorough understanding of this power. That is why the brochures and postcards he photographed of Wildwood (and many other resorts around the country) had the ability to "speak to you." The precision he honed came from his engineering background and training at Rensselaer Polytechnic Institute. It would serve him well. There was not anything he could not design or build to perfect the way in which he performed his job. After graduating, he journeyed in his brother's printing business in Florida, which convinced him that he could succeed in that business as well (making postcards). The rest, as they say, is history.

"When I talk to people in Wildwood now, they say, 'Oh, your Dad was that crazy guy with the funny car,' "explains Eric Bard, David's son, who now runs the business. Funny car, perhaps. Crazy? Yeah, like a fox. When David Bard founded Aladdin Business Service in 1956 in Philadelphia, he did not have any idea of the legacy he was creating. He was (like the rest of Wildwood's "imagineers" - as they say in Disney), doing his job to the best of his ability - and then some.

David created what is arguably some of the finest examples of postcard photography in all of Wildwood, if not the country. His attention to detail, his knack for lighting, his ability to pose strangers and compose sets all added to his advantage over the competition. What he did not realize at the time was that he was capturing a way of life and a slice of vacationing heaven that would be forever frozen in time. What began as humble photographs ended up being journalistic testaments to a lifestyle that has since passed into the annals of history.

Bonito Motel 236 Spicer Avenue, Wildwood. It still has a beautiful sign, albeit a different one. Yet, the property bears little resemblance to this gem of the '60s. Courtesy of ©Aladdin Color Inc. www.RetroStockPix.com

Attaché Motel, 5711 Ocean Avenue, Wildwood Crest. The motel is impeccable in its style. The signature jagged roofline is DooWop royalty. The motel has opted for more muted colors than this Technicolor palette of the '60s. Courtesy of ©Aladdin Color Inc. www.RetroStockPix.com

Imperial 500 Motel, 6601 Atlantic Ave. ,Wildwood Crest. Some of the greatest railings in DooWop architecture. As well appointed today, as it was in this photo. Courtesy of © Aladdin Color Inc. www.RetroStockPix.com

El Ray Motel 4711Atlantic Avenue, Wildwood. Courtesy of © Aladdin Color Inc. www.RetroStockPix.com

Hialeah Motel. 6221 Atlantic Ave., Wildwood. Note David Bard's funky little Beetle in the parking lot. (Motel now demolished). Courtesy of © Aladdin Color Inc. www.RetroStockPix.com

His images depict Wildwood motels showing "movies" on their terraces, or the coffee shop at The Eden Roc with elevated booths that sat flush against the outside windows for all to see the occupants within! Or The Ranch House Motel (mirroring the 50s and 60s obsession with cowboys and Indians) with their sun deck teepees, Conestoga Wagon, and post and rail wooden fence instead of a metal railing. The beauty parlor at the Pan Am is a treasure to see, as well as the wide variety of "additional information" signage that any given hotel featured, such as: efficiency units, air conditioning, heated pool, TV and Hi-Fi, Snack Bar and Beach Pool. Did I mention The Crusader's sauna baths?

Now in his 80s and wintering in Boynton Beach, Florida, and summering in New Paltz, New York, he is lucky to have escaped the sight of seeing the places he so painstakingly tried to promote in their heyday pass into motel memories. However, the fruits of his labors live on in images of a decade past, so stellar, and so captivating, that one just marvels at their beauty and detail.

Like the other Wildwood "greats," it started out as being, "just a living" to David. Eric describes how his Dad got most of those incredible shots, "Well, he had a Volkswagen Beetle (not exactly what one would call a large car), on which he created a 'flat wooden rack' on the roof. There were two metal racks on the roof that held the wooden platform that he would stand on. The 'rack' held a 10 foot ladder, whose back legs were permanently secured to the rack with a stationary metal rod that skewered both legs, also allowing the ladder to pivot."

The Crown Motel with its paneled lobby and tribute to Hollywood stars on the wall. Louisville Ave. & the Ocean, Wildwood Crest. Courtesy of © Aladdin Color Inc. www. RetroStockPix.com

La Vita Resort Motel, 3400 Atlantic Ave. Wildwood Crest. Courtesy of © Aladdin Color Inc. www.RetroStockPix.com

Eric continues, "He would park this car in the middle of the street to sweep above the parking lots of the motels and give him the ability to shoot the pool. However, keep in mind, being in the middle of the street, on top of a 10-foot pivoting ladder, on the roof of your Volkswagen Beetle was a bit dangerous. Therefore, like all good engineers, he added a series of red flashing lights all around the car to alert other vehicles of his presence. But it gets better still," Eric says laughing. "He also added loudspeakers to the car, tied into a hand-held microphone. With this, he had the ability to give directions to us (his able-bodied assistants/children) from a full block away. It was not unusual to hear something like, 'Maid cart on the third floor - please remove it.' All over the loudspeakers, of course."

Eric also speaks of his Dad's methodical manner in which he approached photographing a motel. Every motel had its own 3 inch x 5 inch index card, outlining motel name, address, list of shots, whether it faced east or west and time of day to shoot it. He also noted that at 3:30 PM, Chuck Schumann's "Big Blue Sightseer" would be coming up the coast and that was a perfect time to capture the people on sundecks (with Chuck's boat in the background - Chuck was a friend).

Good equipment was a must and David recognized this fact. He used a 4 x 5 Graflex view camera to capture his images initially, then eventually scaled down to a 2 ¼ format. The large format provided an image of depth and detail that today's digital cameras can only wish for in their dreams. He used Kodachrome and Ektachrome transparency film for their rich vibrancy and knack for capturing "pools of color."

"We always shot four basic images for the postcards—the exterior during the day, the exterior during the night, the guest room and the pool or activity area," says Eric. "Prep time for the whole motel took about 15 minutes. Prep in the guest room consisted of retrieving a box of vases containing brightly colored plastic flowers from the trunk of the Beetle and placing the vases in the rooms to dress them up. We placed them on tables, on dressers, on nightstands - anywhere that needed a splash of color. We made sure all the bedspreads were clean, smooth, corners tucked and edges 'kissed' the floor. We turned the TV on to a talk or game show, because the heads moved slower and were easier to capture on film with a flash. We made sure the curtains were parallel, all the lights were on, and set any kitchenette tables."

Eric, smiling, continues, "Now the pool area was a bit more challenging because that almost always involved hotel guests that we used as models. However, before we shot the people we needed to round up the wet towels on railings. Open all the umbrellas, straighten the chaises and cushions, hide the maids' carts in the stairwells, remove trashcans and most importantly blow up the beach balls and flotation devices for our models to hold!"

"In a pinch, my Dad would take advantage of the fact that he had three boys, a girl, a wife and a gold convertible which he could use as 'substitutions' for models (hotel guests), if need be. If you saw all of us in the foreground, you knew it was an 'ugly week' at the shore. As many of the guests were French Canadian (and spoke French), this presented a bit of a dilemma. Many did not speak very much English and dad did not speak any French. So, I would watch him, as he would 'demonstrate' poses to the ladies with one leg arched and a hand fetchingly held behind his head! He would do the same with the men - nice masculine poses. It was hilarious."

It was not only that people that sometimes presented challenges, it was also the background of the motels and the weather. Eric adds, "Sometimes a small motel had a towering hotel behind it, or some obstruction that would ruin the look of the photo. That is where our 'stripper' came in. He was a person who would cut though the four layers of the film (effectively cutting out all which was undesirable) and added a crystal blue sky to the background. The problem was, this type of work needed to be done in a straight line. It was great for horizons, but when you had to cut around trees, it looked goofy."

Eric calculates that from 1956 to 1991 his father accumulated the monumental stockpile of some 100,000 images, now all archived off-site.

What was the most valuable postcard his Dad ever created? "Well, that's a good question," says Eric. "But I can tell you that after they tore down the Rio Motel, I listed its card on EBay and it sold very quickly!"

If Eric had to choose just one memory of his dad and their Wildwood days together, "It was that ladder. Definitely the ladder," laughs Eric. "This time it was a 15-foot ladder. When my Dad wanted to get a shot of the motel from the ocean - you guessed it - we waded into the gray Atlantic up to our chests with cameras and ladder in tow. I would hold the ladder as my Dad climbed it with the camera and took the shot. More often than not, a huge wave would come by and wipe the ladder and us out. The only image I remember was my Dad's hands held high above the waves (no head visible) with the camera clinched in them. He never lost a camera."

Coral Sands Motel, 5611 Atlantic
Ave., Wildwood. It is now
the annex to the Aztec Motel.
Courtesy of © Aladdin Color Inc.
www.RetroStockPix.com

Jolly Roger 6805 Atlantic Ave., Wildwood
Crest. The architecture of the lobby is
pretty much the same, but the swingin'
furniture is no more. Courtesy of © Aladdin
Color Inc. www.RetroStockPix.com

Casa Bahama Motel,
7301 Atlantic Ave.,
Wildwood Crest.
Courtesy of © Aladdin
Color Inc. www.
RetroStockPix.com

Wildwood: Presented in Technicolor

A Photographic Essay

Golden Railing Motel, 1702 Ocean Ave., North Wildwood. As its name
implies, the stairs & railings glow in the morning sunlight like Inca gold.

The following tribute is proof positive that the details count. The curve of a balcony rail, the slope of a roofline, the fins jutting out between the rooms, or the cantilever deck overhanging the parking lot. The glorious pools are almost decadent in their beauty when one of the greatest beaches of the Atlantic is footsteps away.

These images themselves are a fleeting moment in time. Captured between 2006 & 2009, I can only hope what beauty I now see remains, and when I return in years to come, the architecture of Wildwood has grown and flourished.

Eden Roc, Atlantic & Bennett Aves., Wildwood. It begs the question, "Which came first? The roofline of the Eden Roc or the fins on a Cadillac?" This motel still wins the race.

Rust never sleeps as the Neil Young song suggests, nor do the ravages of the salt air on the tin can of neon signs.

A multi-story tile mural of this valiant Crusader flanks the outer wall of his namesake, the Crusader Motel at Cardinal Rd. & Beach Rd. in Wildwood Crest.

George Jetson's hover car would seem at home parked under the carport of the Brigadoon Motel at 1605 Ocean Ave. in North Wildwood. Named after a Broadway musical about a magical Scottish village, this motel could have just as easily been the Spaceport Inn.

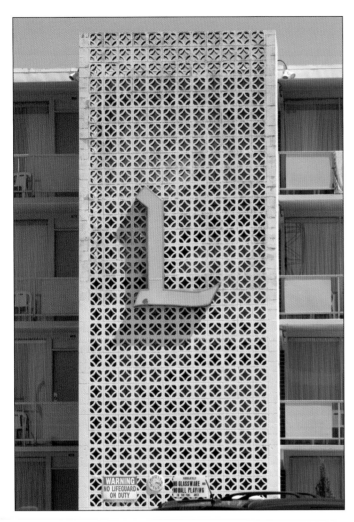

The decorative architectural concrete block of motels like The Landmark in downtown Wildwood, and the Park Lane in the Crest, provides privacy while letting light stream in.

The Park Lane.

The Bristol Plaza Resort Motel made every effort to impress when it was built. The fins on the upper side of the building combined with black lava rock along the lower deck to meld for a tropical twist. Located at 6407 Ocean Avenue, Wildwood Crest.

The stories of runaway luggage carts and skateboarding teens on the ramp at the Caribbean Motel are legendary. A more sedate pursuit, is simply a father trying to keep up with his young son racing back to their room. Located at 5600 Ocean Ave. in Wildwood Crest.

The lounge at the Caribbean with its canted glass walls is best photographed in its daytime glow and best enjoyed as a window on the world when the sun sets and the neon beckons. 5600 Ocean Ave., Wildwood Crest.

The Chateau Bleu is a brilliant white comet in the afternoon sun. Asymmetrical space-age prows cap its porte cochere. Located in North Wildwood at 911 Surf Avenue.

Living out of a suitcase while on vacation has a special charm at the Suitcase Motel in North Wildwood at 1500 New Jersey Avenue. The modern homage to tourist cabin chic makes every room seem like it has a private porch. Stylized shutters in turquoise compliment the matching diamond pattern doors & the greenery adjoining them.

Streamline your need for signage, like that of the Surf Comber Motel. The neon attached directly to the stucco wall works quite nicely on this motel at 4800 Atlantic Ave. in Wildwood.

The airplane-wing roofline of the Ocean View Resort Motel reminds one of the lobby of the classic Satellite Motel. 7201 Ocean Ave., Wildwood Crest.

A Hollywood Squares effect of the balconies at Montego Bay Resort is
along the final stretch of boardwalk in North Wildwood. 1800 Boardwalk.

The triangular deck of the Bristol looks left to the Atlantic Ocean and right down Ocean Avenue.

These railings look like wood, but are actually cast concrete.
The Casa Del Sol at 4109 Ocean Ave. in Wildwood.

The Florentine Motel in North Wildwood is rare in its more costly brick façade. Vertical fenestrations jut out, providing a little privacy as you peek out the door in the morning in just a towel.

A shiny diversion from picking the right motel, this vintage
Airstream trailer is adjacent to the Starlux Hotel parking lot.

The Singapore Motel is a great exception to the rule book. Classic Asian influences enhance its international mystique. Located at 515 E. Orchid Rd. in Wildwood Crest.

In 2006, the umbrellas at the StarLux played with the lines of the hotel in a most interesting way.

The bulge-type guardrail at the Imperial 500 in Wildwood Crest has a "super wow" factor.

The lobby of the Tangiers Resort is more tropical than North African in design. Located at 6201 Atlantic Avenue, Wildwood Crest.

And We'll Have Fun, Fun, Fun!:

Dan MacElrevey

Vintage view of the Surfside Restaurant when it operated from 1963-2002 at 5601 Ocean Ave. in Wildwood Crest. Photo courtesy of © Aladdin Color Inc. www. RetrostockPix.com

The Doo Wop sign garden is one development in Wildwood I hope keeps expanding. Rather than "moth ball" the old motel signs, The Doo Wop Preservation League is relighting the night sky in front of the museum with historic neons of bygone motels.

Sporting the dashing good looks of a sea captain, Dan MacElrevey, took the reigns of president of the Doo Wop Preservation League over from Jack Morey in 2004. As partner and co-founder of Ocean Property Management, his immediate goals for the League were not only about preservations of the buildings, but also preservation of the "lifestyle" and character that came from this post-war community. It was important to him that Wildwood retains the flavor it had captured of the 1950s and 1960s.

"Wildwood is an intergenerational experience," explains Dan. "It is not uncommon for grandparents to have vacationed here, followed by their children and their children's children. It is a family thing. Other manufacturers produce tangible products like cars or computers. The product that we produce is fun and memories," says Dan. No one who has ever been to Wildwood can argue with that sentiment.

As president of the Doo Wop Preservation League, Dan is very cognizant of the fact that much of the city has disappeared. Even, in spite of the valiant efforts of the Doo Wop Preservation League. He views the teardown in two distinct ways. "The initial teardown was a situation where older owners were offered large sums of money by developers and they saw the opportunity to move. You were 70 years old, had a property worth $1 million and you are offered $5 million for it? They saw it as an opportunity to get out and relax on the beaches of Florida.

The other group of people here in Wildwood would not sell their properties for $100 million. They are the types who chase the developers out of their offices - and into the parking lots! They realize what is here and want to preserve it at all costs. A good example is Joe Salerno over at The Imperial 500. His parents built the place. Then they sold it to their son Joe, who recently sold it to his daughter and her husband. Now they are doing many improvements to the building, etc. Lots of expansion."

An ad in the June 2007 edition of *The Sun By-The-Sea* newspaper lists in their real-estate section, a "24 Unit Motel" for sale. It goes on to say, "With pool and hot tub—near shopping and dockside restaurants." $1.9 million.

Also, with the incentives to 'Doo Wop' your property come many benefits. "Doo Wop motels/hotels all sit back from the street. It creates an 'open' feeling. You can add two floors to that building, but still only need one parking place per unit, instead of two. The Shalimar did something interesting. When they went from a 3-story to a 5-story hotel, they added stairs between the units on top of them (making them a two-floor unit). Another interesting fact about The Shalimar was when they did the reconstruction on it; they could not locate the original size exterior tiles any more. Therefore, they hired a person to custom cut those tiles you see all over the building. All winter long this man's only job was to cut tiles."

The Doo Wop museum itself is an artifact. When the owner of the Surfside Restaurant served his final meal there in 2002, he offered the structure to the museum. Dismantled, restored and reassembled on its current Ocean Avenue site, the museum is both full of artifacts and delicious ice cream specialties, served at the counter of Doo Wop Malt Shop.

The dynamic duo of Chuck Schumann and Dan MacElrevey keep the Doo Wop Preservation League a living entity in Wildwood. Rather than just mine treasures from closing motels, the league's support of thriving motels keeps the Wildwoods themselves the real museum.

According to Dan, one big reason Wildwood is experiencing re-growth and new success is the tourism tax they added. The city planners knew that monies generated from a tax (and funneled back to Wildwood, not Trenton) would greatly aid the city. "We allocate more money for tourism than the State of New Jersey allocates for itself. The only other venue in the state that outspends us is Atlantic City. We use that money for advertising and for events. In October, we had a 50s weekend with 6400 people in attendance at the Convention Center. All of those people had to stay and eat somewhere too. And usually, during that time of year, it would have been a 'dead' fall weekend for Wildwood."

"We also use South Beach (Miami, Florida) as a model. South Beach has preserved many of its older hotels and has built newer ones in the art deco style. It's a mix of the best of what we were and the best to come, but always resort-based."

The Shore Diner Sign hangs high above the floor at the DooWop Museum. The sign is a real stunner, but it lived its life off island on Route 9 in Rio Grande .The hand painted gem still makes you salivate for meatloaf and mashed potatoes.

The White Star Motel Sign is not the victim of a teardown. Every once in awhile, a motel recasts itself with a new name. In this case, it is now the Blue Palms.

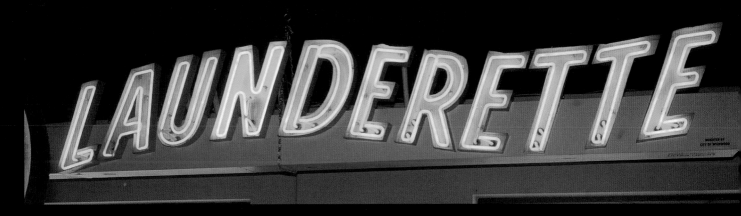

Launderette Sign

Dan says that the toughest period for Wildwood was 1986 to 1988. Many of the motels during that time were taken over by banks. In fact, Ocean Property Management managed the motels at the behest of the banks. "A famous saying in Wildwood at the time was, 'Wildwood has seen its best days'. At that time, the Moreys owned property in California, Utah and other places. Their organization was going to be much larger, because their father and uncle had a vision. However, Will and Jack decided to put that money into Wildwood and pulled out of all of those other places. They decided to invest $20 million on a new roller coaster and boardwalk improvements. They made it better than it ever was. They also brought in renowned architect Steve Izenour - who really changed things. They really put their money where their mouth was, so to speak."

Dan adds with a sly smile, "Doo Wop pays when Doo Wop succeeds."

Marine Italian Bakery

Fly Me to the Moon:

The Future and Beyond

This Wawa narket, built in 2003 on the Rio Grande Avenue Gateway to Wildwood, is unique. From the canopy over its fuel pumps to its oversized neon sign, this convenience oasis screams that DooWop architecture is far from over.

As we round the first decade of the new millennium, Wildwood's future looks bright and promising. The retention of an historic district seemingly is in place, and the anticipation of attracting more 'retro-themed' businesses into Wildwood seems attainable. Over the course of the last decade, many inroads have been made in this positive direction.

The DooWop Museum (a.k.a. The Doo Wop Experience), housed within the salvaged old Surfside Diner, has risen again as part of a larger complex just off the Rio Grande Gateway. The Museum's multi-prowed (or, as I like to call it, crinkle-cut) roof beckons visitors from seemingly all sides. The exterior boasts a 'sign garden' - a mini tour of some of the most prolific of all Wildwood motel signs, The Satellite Motel, The Cavalier, The Swan and The White Star - all struggle for their little patch of fame in front of the museum. Inside, you get "Zaberized" with the famous sign from the landmark restaurant that once anchored North Wildwood's Inlet. Enjoy a 'malted' as you browse through Doo Wop collectibles and admire the vignettes of Americana in the 1950's.

Across the street from the museum sits the gleaming new Wildwood Convention Center, an engineering marvel all its own! The Convention Center boasts 260,000 total square feet of space and literally sits right next to the boardwalk (on the ocean side)!

T.D. Bank, the next-door neighbor of the Wawa market, has a three-dimensional sign that is an homage to the great mouse trap and coaster rides of the Wildwood piers.

More Deco than Doo Wop, the Harley-Davidson dealership on Rio Grande Avenue evokes the look and feel of a vintage 1930s movie palace. Its style dovetails perfectly with the architectural renaissance of Wildwood.

The Subway sign was recast for Wildwood and it found its way back off the island to Subway locations throughout the region. Just off the beach on Rio Grande Avenue, this national chain had the courage to have fun with its logo and discover magic in the process.

The Marvis Diner is retro and 21ˢᵗ century blended seamlessly.
It is located at 4900 Pacific Ave. in Wildwood.

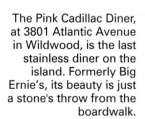

The Pink Cadillac Diner, at 3801 Atlantic Avenue in Wildwood, is the last stainless diner on the island. Formerly Big Ernie's, its beauty is just a stone's throw from the boardwalk.

Cool Scoops is on 1111 New Jersey Ave. in North Wildwood. Set away from the hustle and bustle, it serves great soda fountain specialties in a collector's dream of memorabilia and delight. From the vintage tail–fin booths to the soda machine doors for the bathrooms, this place is in overdrive.

Park Doo Wop. There are several of these signs that "tip the hat" to the past while they lure you into the lot.

Acme Markets. What is old is new again. The logo was a good one the first time around and evokes a simpler past.

Walgreen's Drug Store, 5000 Park Ave., Wildwood. The sign's look is retro but the engine under the hood is state of the art L.E.D. lighting technology. The glow of neon can never be replaced but this sign gives it some serious competition.

Start your engines! The Daytona Motor Inn, 4010 Atlantic Ave., Wildwood.

Kahuna's Bar & Grill, 3817 Pacific Ave., Wildwood.

Mr. D's. The sign is simple magic but the cheese steaks are a piece of heaven. A terrific gallery of neon sign images graces the walls as you wait for your order.

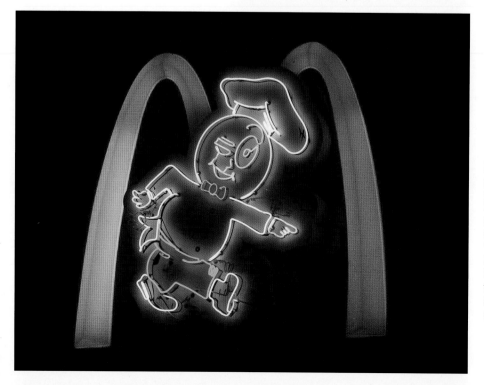

McDonalds on the Boardwalk grabs its own piece of the past with this tribute to its Downey, California, location and the mother of all neon signs. The McDonalds of 1960 was a pretty Doo Wop kind-of-place. I challenge McDonald's to build a glazed-tiled, golden-arched tribute in a place where it would never get old, Wildwood.

The Caribbean Motel has a nice smaller sign near the office,
which sneaks in the number-one deal breaker for guests of
the new millennium. Do you have Wi-Fi buddy?

The eyeball streetlights along Rio Grande Avenue say
Wildwood is a treasure, but it is still first and foremost fun.

Not a sign or even a building, this mini mural on a bike at the Harley-Davidson dealership is a sweet tribute to the Wildwood boardwalk.

Several new establishments have come to Wildwood and have chosen to adopt the "Doo Wop" theme. Among them, a one-of-a kind Wawa (convenience store/gas station) featuring phenomenal neon signage, a 'diagonal' (tilted) roof over the gas pumps and a stainless steel décor. Next door is the T.D. Bank that sports a sign designed to look like a looping roller coaster! Not to mention a great new Walgreens also donning a more classic neon hybrid sign!

Acme Markets has also opted to go "Doo Wop" and created a retro look for their supermarket. The neon sign even boasts a throwback Acme logo from the 1950s.

Subway sandwich shops created a classic neon recreation sign to lure its diners across the street from the stunning Starlux Hotel. This sign has become so popular that they are using it for other locations throughout the country. Just down the street is a Harley Davidson dealership, which is housed in a building made to look like an old movie theater, slathered in foaming aqua and beige tones, complete with a neon marquee.

The Marvis Diner is so popular because of its appearance. It has been selected for film shoots when motion picture companies are in town filming.

The Shalimar Motel in Wildwood Crest has just finished a massive renovation, with the assistance of architect Richard Stokes. They have created a stunning example of what can be accomplished with an existing vintage property when the right design and restoration techniques are applied to it.

Other places, such as the Cool Scoops Ice Cream Parlor, create their own Disney atmosphere with fabulous memorabilia inside and the opportunity to eat your banana splits and smoothies in the back seats of "new" classic cars. The 'eye candy' in Cool Scoops is worth the visit alone! Classic soda fountain memorabilia is everywhere and even the bathroom doors are made out of the fronts of old soda vending machines!

North Wildwood's inlet boasts The Star Diner, replete with its curved walkways, rounded corners, retro Jadeite green color and glitzy neon signage. The food they serve is definitely out-of-this-world, as any patron will tell you (and the line out the door will confirm)!

The crowning jewel of the "new Doo Wop" properties is the shimmering Starlux Hotel. With its cylindrical stairwell, splashy décor, ramped-roof lounge and glittering, knock-it-out-of-the-ballpark sign, she sits at the top of Rio Grande Avenue as a testament of what is to come, not what has been lost. The Starlux may soon be joined by another "family member," as Jack Morey's organization is working on a new hotel property with a boardwalk theme!

Yet, while I am excited for the future of Wildwood, the past always pulls me back like the memories of a youthful summer lost long ago.

The Wildwood of my youth is certainly different from the Wildwood of my adulthood. Then again, so is everything else that I remember. It is often difficult to accept the fact that change is the only constant in all of our lives. Yet, Wildwood has come full circle. Just like a kid growing up, it led a charmed youth, had some very difficult teenage years and finally is enjoying a more sedate, family-oriented adulthood. It is my hope, that with the turbulent years behind her, this beautiful, enchanting, mesmerizing, one-of-a kind place can remain a haven for all of our children (and their children) to enjoy and love.

Wildwood is a place devoid of attitude; it is what it is and wears it proudly. There are few places you can go that will embrace you as Wildwood does. In Wildwood, you can be who you truly are, not some figment of your alter-ego. It does not put on airs or have an inflated opinion of itself. Wildwood is a "real" place, filled with "real" people. That is a very refreshing change these days.

Whether you are speaking to dedicated volunteers or the captains of industry, everyone treats you the same in Wildwood. They give you the time of day. They give you respect and they do not trip over their egos in the process. Few places can offer such realism.

Many of my memories of Wildwood are thankfully unbeknownst to my parents, with my father now, sadly, deceased and my mother in her twilight years. I still remember those days and nights vividly. Just like everyone else who ever walked that same boardwalk of life from youth to young adulthood, Wildwood was an integral part of that passage. I still smile every time we pass The Summer Sands (now a condominium), and yearn for The Cavalier, The Hialeah, The Tides, and The Catalina.

Murals are sneaking up on the blank canvases of many a Wildwood motel.
The Aztec mural blends seamlessly with its two treasured signs.

Jolly Roger Motel, 6805 Atlantic Ave., Wildwood Crest.

Years later, I returned to the somewhat subdued glitz and glamour of Wildwood with my then-young son, Gregory, to "show him the lights of Ocean Avenue." He was equally mesmerized. Like me, he too always begged to go "to the Boardwalk." And I, knowing just what a life-altering experience that can be for a kid, did not have the heart to deny him that experience.

Those wild ladies wave goodbye after an adventure in Wildwood. They pass the Eden Roc at 5201 Atlantic Ave. in Wildwood. Courtesy of © Aladdin Color Inc. www.RetroStockPix.com

"See you in September.
See you when the summer's through..."

Bibliography

Books

Francis, David W., Diane DeMali Francis, and Robert J. Scully, Sr. *Wildwoods By-The-Sea*. Fairview Park, OH: Amusement Park Books, Inc.,1998.

Futrell, Jim. *Amusement Parks of New Jersey.* Mechanicsburg, PA :Stackpole Books, 2004.

Hastings, Kirk. *Doo Wop Motels: Architectural Treasures of The Wildwoods*. Mechanicsburg, PA :Stackpole Books, 2007

Heimann, Jim, and Heller, Steven. Shop America. Mid-Century Storefront Design, 1938-1950. Los Angeles, CA: Taschen, 2007.

Hess, Alan. *Googie Redux: Ultramodern Roadside Architecture*. San Francisco, CA: Chronicle Books, 2004.

Hine, Thomas. *Populuxe.* New York, NY: The Overlook Press, 1986.

Hirsch, Michael Loren, and Richard Stokes, and Anthony Bracali. *How to Doo Wop: Wildwoods-By-The-Sea Handbook of Designs Guidelines.*

Lapidus, Morris. *Too Much Is Never Enough.* New York, NY: Rizzoli, 1996.

Martino, Vincent, Jr. The Wildwoods: 1920-1970. Charleston, SC: Arcadia, 2007.

Salvini, Emil R. *The Summer City By The Sea: Cape May, New Jersey, An Illustrated History.* New Brunswick, NJ: Rutgers University Press, 1995.

Venturi, Robert, Denise Scott Brown, and Steven Izenour. *Learning From Las Vegas.* MA: Massachusetts Institute of Technology, 1977.

Williams, Robert. *Hometown Diners.* New York, NY: Harry N. Abrams, 1999.

Wright, Jack. *Fab~O~Rama!: The Story of Morey's Piers, Planet Earth's Greatest Seaside Amusement Park.* Cape May, NJ: Exit Zero Publishing, 2009.

Film

"Wildwood Days." Producer Carolyn Travis. Travisty TV Productions, 2004.

"Field of Dreams." Producer Lawrence Gordon. Universal Studios, 1989.

"Doo Wop Motels." Producer Dan Espy. Espy Media Group, 2006.

"The Jetsons." Producer Hanna-Barbera. ABC Television, 1962-1963.

"The Wonder Years." Producer The Black-Marlens Company. ABC Television, 1988-1993.

Magazines

Southgate, Martha. " A Different World." *Print Magazine,* Feb. 2009.

Strauss, Robert. " Power Issue: Will and Jack Morey." *NJ Monthly,* 9 Dec. 2008.

Williams, Melinda M. and Robert O. Williams. "Those Wildwood Days." *Sign Builder Illustrated*, April 2006.

Williams, Melinda M. and Robert O. Williams. "Rediscovering Neon." *Sign Builder Illustrated,* December 2006.

Newspapers

The Sun By-the-Sea 2006 to present.

Goldstein, Steve and Jacqueline L. Urgo. " Tacky Motels? No, Treasures." *The Philadelphia Inquirer,* 11 May 2006.

Songs

The Tempos, "See You In September." 1959.

Garfield, Gil and Perry Botkin, Jr., "Wonderful Summer," 1963-1964.

Howard, Bart. "Fly Me To the Moon," 1954.

The Guess Who, "American Woman," 1968.

Lou Reed, "Walk On The Wild Side," 1977.

The Drifters, "Under the Boardwalk," 1964.

Brian Wilson and Mike Love, "Fun, Fun, Fun," 1964.

Paul Simon, "Kodachrome,"1973.

Websites

Kramer, Doug. "Rancho Style," Doug Kramer's Rancho Style. 2004-2005, www.ranchostyle.com/cliffnotes. html